CHAMPIONS OF FAITH

Great Stories VOLUME 1 of the Bible

BOLD ADVENTURERS

Merlin L. Neff

Pacific Press® Publishing Association
Nampa, Idaho
Oshawa, Ontario, Canada
www.pacificpress.com

Cover design by Gerald Lee Monks
Cover illustration by Clyde Provonsha
Inside design by Steve Lanto

All Scriptures quoted are from The New King James Version,
copyright © 1979, 1980, 1982, Thomas Nelson, Inc., Publishers.

Library of Congress Cataloging-in-Publication Data

Neff, Merlin L.
Bold adventurers / Merlin L. Neff.
p. cm. — (Champions of faith ; #1)
ISBN-13: 978-0-8163-2264-0 (hardcover)
ISBN-10: 0-8163-2264-3 (hardcover)
1. Bible stories, English. 2. Bible—Biography—Juvenile literature.
I. Title.
BS551.3.N44 2008
220.9'505—dc22

2007052274

Additional copies of this book are available by calling toll-free
1-800-765-6955 or by visiting http://www.adventistbookcenter.com.

08 09 10 11 12 • 5 4 3 2 1

"Train up a child in the way he should go, and when he is old he will not depart from it."

—Proverbs 22:6

Interior illustrations:

Robert Ayres: pages 16, 17, 124, 128.
Joe Maniscalco: pages 20, 60, 64, 69, 76, 80, 81, 88, 89, 92, 93, 100, 108, 121, 136, 139, 155.
Clyde Provonsha: pages 8, 9, 12, 13, 28, 32, 33, 37, 40, 41, 45, 49, 52, 105.
John Steel: pages 21, 24, 25, 48, 56, 57, 113, 117, 148.
Helen Torrey: page 96.

CONTENTS

FOR PARENTS

**Pass Your Values On to Your Children
Through Bible Stories**

As a parent, you likely want your nine- or ten- or eleven-year-old daughter or son to enter the teen years knowing the most important stories of the Bible. As you look for ways to pass on to your child the love of God and the principles that represent His character, consider how well a good story captures the attention of human beings of all ages. The Bible stories in these five volumes will place God's principles in your child's mind in such a way that they won't forget them as they grow older.

Read these books with your child—or have the child read the story to you—morning or evening or Sabbath afternoon, every week. This is a good way to build your child's character and faith in God without your having to explain a bunch of abstract ideas. Their awareness of how God works with His people will grow without their realizing it.

Every generation through history that forgot about the Scriptures, and therefore the knowledge and implementation of God's principles, has suffered greatly from its own evil and self-destructive actions. A similar destiny awaits the children of this generation if we fail to bring the stories of the Bible to bear on their lives. The stakes are too high, the dangers too close, for us to neglect the story of salvation as we raise our children.

The timeless truths of the Bible come through clearly in the stories of this five-volume set. Each story has been screened for some elements more suited to adult readers. The stories chosen are the ones that follow the thread of salvation down through the centuries. In places where people of the Bible speak to each other, the words are quoted from the New King James Version, which is fairly easy to understand and widely accepted.

Pray for your child that he or she will respond positively when the Holy Spirit speaks to his or her heart. These Bible stories may bring your child to a turning point of knowing God in their own experience and accepting His love and His principles for themselves. There is supernatural power in the Word of God that may change your son or daughter forever.

The Publisher

A WORLD GOD MADE

Genesis 1; 2

We love to go back to the beginning of things. We want to know, how did they start? Let's say that we see a sturdy, wide-spreading oak tree in a meadow. It has stood through storms and winds for almost a hundred years. But how did it begin? Where did it come from?

You spot a tiny acorn under the tree and find that it holds the secret of the oak. The brown acorn, cold and hard, almost like a rock, has fallen to the ground. The sunshine and rain work on the acorn, and soon the life hidden within its shell sends out shoots that eventually grow into another strong oak tree.

Or say we see a caterpillar crawling across a leaf on a shrub. Day after day we see it as we walk by. It changes into a hard, wrinkled cocoon. Then one warm morning we discover life stirring in this crinkly lump, and soon a gorgeous butterfly comes out and dries its silky wings in the sun.

Life is a strange mystery. How is life hidden in the acorn? How does the caterpillar produce a perfect butterfly? Where did life come from in the first place?

Let's go back to the time when there was no life on this earth. We will start at the beginning of our world. "In the beginning God created the heavens and the earth. The earth was without form, and void; and darkness was on the face of the deep. And the Spirit of God was hovering over the face of the waters." Yes, our earth was a dark planet with water on the surface, with no plants or animals. What a strange, dismal picture—no life, no moving creatures, no sound, no light!

Then the wise, loving God in heaven began to make the world into a beautiful home in which people and animals could live. As He thought about the world in darkness, He commanded, "Let there be light." When He spoke, rays of light broke through the blackness; more and more light shone upon the water-covered earth. This was the first morning of the world's history. However, if we could have looked at this scene, we would not have thought it was an attractive place for a home, not yet. God saw the light and called it Day, and the darkness He called Night.

On the second day God spoke again, and the water on the earth was separated from the water above the earth.

The clear blue dome of the sky appeared, and God called it the heavens. We know that the sky is filled with air, called the atmosphere, that reaches above the earth's surface for miles, and that the water in the atmosphere is carried in clouds that you see floating in the air.

As the second day of Creation closed, the earth had fresh air and light. Since both of these are necessary for plants and animals to live, we can see how God was preparing a home for human beings.

On the third day God said, "Let the waters under the heavens be gathered together into one place, and let the dry land appear." Then the waters on the earth rolled and tumbled together to become oceans; and dry land rose up above the seas for the first time. The hills stood out tall and majestic, and the valleys and plains were spread over the earth; but the hills and plains were not yet beautiful, because they were just dirt.

You may have seen the bare earth left behind after a river has overflowed its banks. The new world without grass or trees must have looked like land that had been flooded. But God continued His work and said, "Let the earth bring forth grass, the herb that yields seed, and the fruit tree that yields fruit according to its kind, whose seed is in itself, on the earth." And it happened that way; the trees, grasses, and plants appeared on the

QUICK FACT:
God created everything in just the right order. He made sure there was air to breathe and grass to eat before He created any cows or horses.

fresh soil that only the day before had been covered with water.

The seeds of plants and grasses that God created always obey the laws of nature, which are God's rules. If we plant beans, they will produce beanstalks and more beans. If we plant corn, then we can expect corn to grow. The seeds produce plants of the same kind.

As God looked at the new world carpeted with green grass and adorned with flowers of every color, as He saw the beautiful trees loaded with fruit, He said that it was all very good!

Trees, grass, and flowers grow best in the sunlight. On the fourth day God caused the sun to appear. Its warm rays shone on the hills and glistened on the rivers flowing through the valleys. In the evening, after the sun had set, the moon and stars appeared. God commanded the sun and moon to give light and also to separate day from night. He said, "Let them be for signs and seasons, and for days and years."

The billions of stars that astronomers have seen and photographed through telescopes are really great big suns

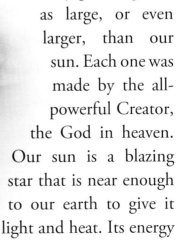

as large, or even larger, than our sun. Each one was made by the all-powerful Creator, the God in heaven. Our sun is a blazing star that is near enough to our earth to give it light and heat. Its energy

makes it possible for plants, animals, and people to live and grow.

We set our clocks by the position of the stars in the heavens. We mark the length of the year by the time it takes for our earth to make a complete trip around the sun. We divide the

THOUGHT QUESTION:

God created human beings "in His own image"–which means He created us to be like Him. In what ways are we like God?

year into months according to the movement of the moon. The sun, moon, and stars are the clock of the heavens to mark off years and months and seasons. They obey the rules of their Creator, and we can depend on them for their precise movement.

On the fifth day God created the fish that live in the seas and rivers; He also made the birds and insects that fly in the air. The new world suddenly came to life with the flash of wings. The fish jumped in the rivers, while bees buzzed and crickets chirped among the flowers and grass. Great whales glided through the sea and spouted when they came to the surface for air. Bluebirds, orioles, parrots, eagles, ducks, pigeons, ostriches—birds of every color and size appeared. Birds with bright-colored plumage perched in the trees, while songbirds made the air ring with sweet sounds—earth's first music. Once more, at the close of the fifth day, God looked on His work and saw that it was good.

On the sixth day God made the land animals and reptiles. Think of the many creatures that roamed the earth that day for the first time! The forests and fields were suddenly alive with elephants, lions, horses, cows, monkeys, kangaroos, moose, and a thousand other animals! Many of the creatures that lived then were much larger than the ones we see today. The bones of giant animals have been found buried in the earth, and you may see some of them in a museum.

The earth, covered with many kinds of grass, magnificent trees, and beautiful flowers, was now filled with the songs of birds and the sounds of the animals. The deer leaped through the grass. The bears climbed up into the trees. The lions roamed about the grasslands. But the animals were not wild or savage as they are today but were gentle and unafraid. Above them was the blue sky and warm sunlight—signs of God's love. But still something was lacking. There were no people to enjoy this perfect home.

God said, "Let Us make man in Our image, according to Our likeness." From the dust of the earth He formed a body in the shape of a man. It was made in the likeness of

GOD SAYS:

"Then God blessed the seventh day and sanctified it, because in it He rested from all His work which God had created and made." -Genesis 2:3

God Himself. Then the Creator breathed into the clay body the breath of life, and there it was: a living human being! He had a perfect head with eyes to see, ears to hear, and a mouth to speak. He had strong arms to carry things and sturdy legs to walk and run wherever he wanted to go. This was truly a wonderful being, made to look like God Himself!

We know today that the chemical elements in the soil are the same as those that we have in our bodies, but only our mighty God could take the soil of the earth, form a man from it, and give him life.

This man was strong and healthy. He could think and speak; he could run; he could swim in the river; he could work. He loved his Creator and listened to all of His instructions. His eyes were sharp; his ears could hear the song of faraway birds and the rustle of the leaves.

Adam, the first man, walked through the forests and along the river. He saw the cheetahs and hippos, the squirrels, the birds in the trees, and the eagle soaring high in the air.

When Adam grew hungry, what should he eat? He remembered that God had said, "Of every tree of the garden you may freely eat; but of the tree of the knowledge of good and evil you shall not eat, for in the day that you eat of it you shall surely die." Perhaps the man saw some

luscious red strawberries and decided to pick one and put it in his mouth. How good it tasted! He picked an orange and sampled its sweet flavor. As he walked under the trees he found walnuts and pecans, which he shelled and ate. The beautiful new world had an abundance of food for people.

Some of the animals followed Adam, and he watched each one. He saw the elephant swing its trunk and look at him with sharp little eyes. The deer was curious and came close to the man. God had all the animals walk past Adam, and he gave names to every one of them. Would you like to have named all the birds and animals? Adam had to think of many names, each of them fit for the creature.

Adam saw that all of the living creatures were in pairs. Not one of them was alone. He began to feel lonely. Was there no one on the earth who could be his companion?

While Adam was considering his situation, God caused him to fall into a deep sleep. Then He opened the man's

side and took out one of his ribs. God formed the rib into another beautiful creature—a woman. Here is a wonderful lesson for us. The woman who becomes the wife of a man stands beside him as his equal. She is not above him and not below him. She is to love her husband and be his faithful companion in life.

God brought the woman to the man, and he loved her, and she became his wife. And Adam gave her the name Eve because she was the mother of all human beings.

At the close of the sixth day God looked over the earth filled with living creatures, which were to be ruled by the man and the woman, and He saw that everything He had made was very good.

The task of creating the world was finished in only six days! God's crowning work was people, who were formed in the image of their Creator. Adam and Eve were given charge over the earth and all the animals in it.

On the seventh day God rested from His work. He made the seventh day of the week a special occasion in honor of the new world He had created. God blessed the seventh day and set it apart from the other six days of the week as a time for people to rest and to remember the One who made the world and created them. We remember the Sabbath, too, because it's the special day of the week when we worship and honor our Creator and thank Him for our beautiful world. We go to church and listen to God's Word on the Sabbath, and we can go out in nature to study His amazing works.

An Enemy in the Garden

Genesis 3

Did Adam and Eve have the whole world for their home? Did they build a house to live in? What was their life like? These are questions we might ask when we read about God's new world and the first man and woman.

When our God, the Creator, made the earth, He planned an ideal home for Adam and Eve. It was called the Garden of Eden. A river flowed through this garden and watered the trees and plants. Adam and his wife would care for the trees, the plants, and the vines, and watch over the animals.

The happy couple did not have a house such as we live in today. The weather was perfect—it wasn't too cold or too hot, nor was there any rain, because "a mist went up from the earth and watered the whole face of the ground." Adam and Eve had a beautiful bower to sleep in. Its walls were climbing vines entwined with fragrant flowers. Birds warbled softly in the branches above them, and soft grass made a living carpet for their feet.

Think of living in a perfect world and discovering the wonders of nature around you. Adam and Eve walked around in their Eden home and watched the strutting peacock on the grass; they laughed as they saw the monkeys swinging in the trees and saw the elephant spray-

ing water over itself with its trunk. The squirrels jumped from limb to limb in the treetops, and tigers, as gentle as lambs, followed them.

Adam and Eve watched the bees making honey and observed the mother kangaroo carrying her baby in her pouch. No doubt they stood on the bank of the river where white swans glided by and quacking ducks fed on the lush grass. Adam must have gathered sweet fruit and nuts from the trees and brought them to his wife. They could sit in the shade and enjoy the fresh delicacies together.

On the seventh day of each week they rested from their work and worshiped God. The Creator talked with Adam and Eve, explaining the wonders of the world to them and telling them how they could continue to be perfectly happy.

Eden had many trees loaded with fruit, and the man and woman had all that they could eat. Only two of the trees in the Garden had special instructions. One tree, called "the tree of life," had rich, life-giving fruit, and God said they could eat as much as they wanted.

Another special tree in the Garden was called "the tree of the knowledge of good and evil." Enticing fruit grew on this tree; but Adam and Eve were told not to eat any of it. The Lord God said to Adam: "Of every tree of the garden you may freely eat; but of the tree of the knowledge of good and evil you shall not eat, for in the day that you eat of it you shall surely die."

God asked the man and woman to trust Him and to obey His words. Surely they loved their Creator enough to keep His rules, for in obeying them they would find true happiness forever. If they wanted their own selfish way, they could do as they pleased; but it would bring them sorrow, pain, and death. Would you have obeyed God if you had lived in that garden home?

One day Eve was walking alone in the Garden, far away from Adam. The serpent—a wise and clever creature—spoke to her from the branches of the tree of the knowledge of good and evil. The woman was surprised and startled to hear this strange, musical voice, so she stopped and looked at the beautiful serpent. It was eating some of the rich-looking fruit of the forbidden tree. Satan, the evil one, who is sometimes called the devil, was talking through the serpent. He asked Eve, "Has God indeed said, 'You shall not eat of every tree of the garden'?"

Eve quickly answered, "We may eat the fruit of the trees of the garden; but of the fruit of the tree which is in the midst of the garden, God has said, 'You shall not eat it, nor shall you touch it, lest you die.'"

"You will not surely die," said the serpent to the woman, "for God knows that in the day you eat of it your eyes will be opened,

QUICK FACT:
In the beginning there was no rain—not until the Flood. Instead, God caused a mist to come up out of the earth to water everything.

and you will be like God, knowing good and evil."

The woman listened to these lying words. She forgot the warning of God, and she looked at the fruit of the tree of the knowledge of good and evil. It seemed to be good to eat. She wondered if God had really meant what He said.

Eve could not take her eyes from the tree. If she could only taste the fruit! She started to pick some of it, but then she drew back. She remembered God's words concerning the fruit of this tree: "You may not eat any of it."

GOD SAYS:

"So when the woman saw that the tree was good for food, that it was pleasant to the eyes, and a tree desirable to make one wise, she took of its fruit and ate." –Genesis 3:6

Then suddenly the serpent picked the fruit and offered it to Eve. "You will be like God, knowing good and evil," he said in her ear. She wanted to be great; she longed to be wise. Perhaps if she ate the fruit, she would be like God. The woman snatched the fruit from the serpent and ate it.

Then Eve thought of Adam, and she picked some of the forbidden fruit and carried it to him, and he ate it. They both knew they had disobeyed God's command, and they felt ashamed.

The Creator had made this tree a test to the man and the woman. If Adam and Eve had truly loved God, they would have obeyed Him and left the fruit of this tree alone. Disobeying God and breaking His rules is called sin. Adam and Eve had committed the first sin.

When evening came, the man and the woman heard the Lord God walking in the Garden. He was looking for them; but Adam and Eve did not want to see God. They hid among the trees, hoping that He would not find them.

"Where are you?" God called to the man.

Adam could not hide when the Lord spoke to him, so he said, "I heard Your voice in the garden, and I was afraid . . . and I hid myself." Adam, created in the image of God, had become afraid of his Creator because he had broken the rule of his new home.

The Lord said, "Have you eaten from the tree of which I commanded you that you should not eat?"

The man hung his head. He did not want to admit he had done wrong, so he tried to excuse himself by saying, "The woman whom You gave to be with me, she gave me of the tree, and I ate."

God turned to Eve. "What is this you have done?" He asked.

Eve did not want to admit her sin either, and she answered, "The serpent deceived me, and I ate."

Because it had spoken the lie of Satan, the serpent was cursed. God said,

> "Because you have done this,
> You are cursed more than all cattle,
> And more than every beast of the field;
> On your belly you shall go,
> And you shall eat dust
> All the days of your life" (Genesis 3:14).

Perhaps this is one reason why snakes are generally feared and hated today.

The Lord God spoke sad words to the man and the woman. He told Eve that she would have pain and sorrow because she disobeyed. He told Adam that his work would be much harder, for now thorns, thistles, and weeds would grow on the earth. He would sweat and grow tired at his labor. Because they had broken the rules of the garden home, the man and woman could no longer enjoy it. They must leave it and go to another part of the world. They could never eat of the special fruit of the tree of life again; they could not sit on the bank of the river of life. Because of their sin they would grow old, and someday they would die.

But the Creator loved Adam and Eve even though they had broken His rules. He gave them a promise that was like a light in deep darkness. He said to Satan,

> "I will put enmity
> Between you and the woman,
> And between your seed and her Seed;
> He shall bruise your head,
> And you shall bruise His heel" (Genesis 3:15).

It meant that there would be conflict between Eve's children and the evil one, and someday Satan would be destroyed. A Hero would be born among the people of the earth, and He would fight the enemy. This Hero would be Jesus, God's only Son, and He would give up His life to gain the victory over Satan.

Adam and Eve could look with hope to the time when Jesus would come from heaven to pay the death penalty for all the sins of humanity. They did not realize He would not come during their lifetime; but the bright promise of a Redeemer would burn in their hearts and the hearts of many faithful people until Jesus came to "save His people from their sins" (Matthew 1:21).

THOUGHT QUESTION: If Adam hadn't eaten the fruit with Eve, would sin have still entered our world?

Now that Adam and Eve were leaving the Garden of Eden, they needed clothing to shield them. They had not needed clothes before because they were perfect and pure. After they sinned, they would need something to cover them and protect them from briers and thorns that were beginning to grow, and to keep out the cold winds. God gave them coats made from the skins of dead animals. His love is wonderful, because He thought of His children's needs and cared for them even though they had disobeyed Him.

It was a sad day when God led the man and woman out of the Garden. No longer could they come and talk with Him as they had in their Eden home. Never again did Adam and Eve walk in that idyllic park God had given them; an angel with a sword of fire stood guard at the entrance.

As the sun set that first evening, tears came into the eyes of the man and the woman. They were beginning to understand how their selfish disobedience had destroyed their happiness.

WHEN CAIN HATED HIS BROTHER

Genesis 4

As Adam and Eve left the gate of the Garden of Eden to seek shelter in the world, they felt sad and lonely. If they had been afraid in their beautiful home after they had broken God's rules, they were much more fearful now in a strange land where they had never been before.

The man and woman needed a place to live, so Adam built a shelter. He found that he had to work hard to get food. Eve saw the first weeds and thorns growing; she watched the first colored leaves fall from the trees, and these reminded her of the blight on nature that was the result of sin.

But in spite of the hardships that came to them, Adam and Eve never forgot God's promise of a Savior. Many times they went back to the gate of the Garden of Eden to worship God.

To help people remember that someday they would be saved from sin, the Lord told Adam to take a lamb from his flock and kill it. The lamb had done no wrong; but

29

when Adam took the life of that innocent creature, he was reminded that sin caused death. He began to wish for the day when Jesus, the Lamb of God, would come to take away the sin of the world.

THOUGHT QUESTION:
Why didn't God accept Cain's offering of fruit?

Wouldn't this be a strange world if it were the home of only two people? God had a plan that many more people should live on the earth. A day came when Eve gave birth to a son. She said, "I have gotten a man from the Lord." The happy mother and father named the baby Cain. They hoped this infant would grow up to be the Hero who would save humanity by overcoming Satan.

As a boy, Cain helped his father plant the seeds and harvest the grain in the field. He listened to the story of the creation of the world from his father, Adam.

After a time, another baby came to the family. Eve named her second son Abel. When the boy grew old enough to go out into the field, he helped his father care for the sheep. Adam told Cain and Abel that God's Son would someday come to earth to save people from sin. When the boys saw their father kill a lamb and offer it as a sacrifice, they understood that it was to remind them of the coming Savior.

When Cain grew older, he decided he wanted to be a farmer. He sowed seeds and cared for the growing plants.

Abel chose to be a shepherd. He cared for his sheep in the rich pasture land not far from his father's home.

A day came when Cain and Abel brought an offering to God. Each of the brothers gathered stones and piled them up to make an altar as their father had done. Cain brought a basket of fruits and grains from his field and his orchard as an offering. He was strong, and he had worked hard. He was proud of his harvest. But he forgot the promise of God and did not bring a lamb as an offering.

Abel loved the Lord and followed His commands. He brought a lamb, killed it, and placed it on his altar. He looked forward to the coming of the Lamb of God, the Savior who was promised to Adam and Eve and who would free them from sin.

Abel's offering pleased the Lord; but Cain's gift was not accepted. And because his offering did not find favor with God, Cain became furious.

God saw him and said, "Why are you angry? And why has your countenance fallen? If you do well, will you not be accepted? And if you do not do well, sin lies at the door. And its desire is for you, but you should rule over it."

By these words Cain knew he had disobeyed; but he was not sorry for his mistake. He was not only angry; he also hated Abel because his offering was accepted.

GOD SAYS:

"And the Lord respected Abel and his offering, but He did not respect Cain and his offering." -Genesis 4:4, 5

Cain allowed this black sin of hatred to grow until it filled his heart. One day the two men were in the field together. Cain quarreled with his younger brother and lost his temper. In his fury, he struck Abel. The younger brother fell to the ground, and he did not move or cry out. He was dead! This was the terrible result of Cain's jealousy and hate. He was afraid because of his terrible sin. He wanted to run away from God, just as his parents, Adam and Eve, had once tried to do in the Garden of Eden.

God spoke to Cain. He asked, "Where is Abel your brother?"

Cain refused to tell what he had done. "I do not know," he lied. "Am I my brother's keeper?"

Cain hoped that God would not know what he had done. He tried to hide his sin by telling a lie. How often when we do something wrong, we try to cover it up by telling a lie, which is another sin. We cannot hide anything from the Lord; He sees what we do and hears every word we speak.

Cain should have been his younger brother's protector and companion. He should have loved him and guarded him from harm. But in anger he killed him instead. God punished Cain for his sin. He told

32

him that he must wander around the earth without friends, because other people would be afraid of him. He would be shunned and despised as a murderer.

Adam and Eve were heartbroken when they found their lifeless son Abel. But tears of grief could not bring Abel back to life. The wages of sin is death. They suffered even more because Abel had been killed by his brother. Adam and Eve could see the results of their own sin in the sorrow that came to their home.

Cain did not want to face his parents any longer, so he left home and wandered away to a land called Nod. Adam and Eve were left alone. They missed Cain, and they mourned for Abel. They often dreamed of the happy days in the Garden of Eden, and they longed to return to that perfect home.

Another son was born to Adam and Eve, and he was named Seth. They had other sons and daughters as the years passed. It is difficult for us to realize how long people lived in those days. Adam was 130 years old when Seth was born. Father Adam was strong, and he lived to see eight generations of children born into the world. Think of nine generations in a family all living at one time! Imagine calling Adam great-great-great-great-great-great-grandfather!

Eve loved her grandchildren and, no doubt, when they were babies, she thought of God's promise and hoped

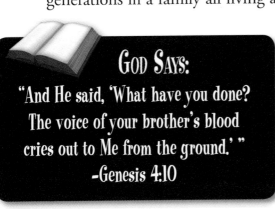

GOD SAYS:
"And He said, 'What have you done? The voice of your brother's blood cries out to Me from the ground.'"
-Genesis 4:10

one of the sons would be the promised Savior. Adam could tell Seth, Enoch, Methuselah, and Lamech many thrilling stories when they were boys. Father Adam was 874 years old when Lamech, the child of the ninth generation, was born. Through the years all

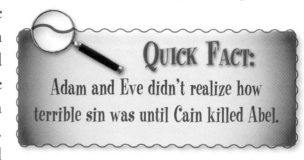

QUICK FACT: Adam and Eve didn't realize how terrible sin was until Cain killed Abel.

of the boys and girls must have listened to Adam's stories about the Garden of Eden and how he had talked with God.

Adam did not die until he was 930 years old. That is almost a thousand years. But one man, Methuselah, lived even longer than Adam.

A FLOOD DESTROYS THE EARTH

Genesis 6–8

As the years passed, more and more people lived on the earth. Those who kept herds of animals settled in the green valleys where the rivers flowed. These shepherds lived in tents made from the skins of sheep and goats. They traveled from place to place so that their flocks could have green pastures and water. Trees, vines, and shrubs made the land look beautiful, although it was not as perfect as the Garden of Eden had been.

Men were skillful in their work. They made tools from brass and iron. They also made harps and other musical instruments for hours of happy entertainment. But they became so wrapped up in their business and pleasure that they forgot God and did not thank Him for food, shelter, and all the good things they had. They thought only of themselves and of eating, drinking, and having a good time. They became lawless in their actions, killing, stealing, and lying to get the things they wanted.

Finally they became so evil that God, who loved His

people, said He was sorry He had created them at all. It was a terrible thing for God's people, who had been made in the image of God Himself, to fall so low in sin!

A few people were loyal to God and obeyed His commandments. Among them was Enoch, who was the seventh generation from

Adam. He probably heard the story of the Garden of Eden directly from Adam.

Although most of the people were selfish and wicked, Enoch was always ready to obey God. He "walked with God" and then, the Bible says, he disappeared from the earth. He did not die like the other people on the earth; he was taken straight to heaven to live with God. Here was a man in a world of sin who lived a pure, honest life. He had walked with God for 365 years before he was taken to heaven.

GOD SAYS:

"Then the Lord saw that the wickedness of man was great in the earth, and that every intent of the thoughts of his heart was only evil continually." -Genesis 6:5

Enoch had a son before he went to heaven, whose name was Methuselah. The son reached the great age of 969 years before he died. Think of living close to a thousand years! Methuselah was the oldest man who ever lived.

When the Lord saw that the wickedness of sinful people was becoming worse and worse, He said, "I will destroy man whom I have created from the face of the earth, both man and beast, creeping thing and birds of the air, for I am sorry that I have made them."

But then He thought of Noah, who was the great-grandson of Enoch. Here was a man who walked with God and obeyed His words. He had a wife and three sons, Shem, Ham, and Japheth.

God told this faithful man Noah that the earth was going

to be destroyed, but he and his family would be saved. Noah was to build an ark, which means a giant boat. God said that a mighty flood of water would destroy every living creature on the earth.

Noah believed what God said, and he began to work on the ark. It was about six hundred feet long, one hundred feet wide, and sixty feet high. It had three decks, and it was made of strong wood covered with black pitch, or tar, inside and out, so that it would not leak.

Noah and his sons worked on the great boat longer than most people live today. Many who lived near Noah watched the shipbuilders at their work. *What is Noah making?* they wondered.

Noah told them he was building an ark, as God had commanded. He told them that the earth was to be destroyed by a flood of water. Furthermore, Noah asked his friends to help build the boat and to come on board when it was ready. There would be room for them if they would accept God's invitation to be saved.

But the neighbors laughed at Noah and said he was foolish. Some of them helped with the building but did not believe that a flood was coming. They had never seen rain, because, as we said before, until that time the earth had always been watered by a mist that came up out of the ground.

As the time drew near when the boat would be finished, Noah begged the people to save themselves from the terrible flood; but men and women refused to believe his warning. They thought the sun would always shine just as it had since they were born.

Noah was not discouraged, because he trusted in God. When the ark was finished, the Lord told Noah to gather food and supplies for his family and for all the animals. Then it was time, God said, for Noah to take his wife and his three sons and their wives and get on board.

Once more Noah invited his neighbors to come with him, but they all refused. God told Noah, "Come into the ark, you and all your household, because I have seen that you are righteous before Me in this generation." Noah and his family left their home for the last time. The crowd laughed as the eight people walked up the gangplank and entered the ark.

Then a strange thing happened. Out of the forests and down from the hills, animals and birds came. Camels and tigers, bears and elk, lions and giraffes, rabbits and wolves, small animals and large moved toward the ark; and yet no man was herding them. With a flutter of wings, flocks of birds darkened the sky. They flew toward the huge boat and found shelter in it. Two of every kind of bird and animal came at God's call. Seven pairs of the animals that are clean to eat, such as sheep and cows, also found safety in the ark. Noah and his descendants would need them for food after the Flood.

What a sight that must have been. Here was the biggest animal parade the world has ever seen! It should have been an important lesson to those who stood watching. The people

41

would not obey God, but the animals answered His call to obey.

The men and women who had laughed at Noah looked on with amazement. Perhaps some of them began to worry a little bit and wished they had gone in with Noah; but no one had the courage to enter the ark.

When all the animals were safely sheltered in the boat, God Himself shut the giant door. The rain did not begin immediately. For seven days the sun continued to shine. The people on the outside laughed at Noah and his family, who were shut up in the ark.

On the eighth day, dark clouds gathered in the sky, lightning flashed, and the storm broke in terrible fury. Water burst up out of the ground in huge torrents and began to fill the valleys. Wind drove the rain in great sheets over the land.

Day and night the water continued to pour from the sky and from under the ground, and the rivers and seas rose higher and higher. The floodwaters destroyed all the homes built in the valleys, and thousands of people ran to the hills and

QUICK FACT:
There was more floor space in the ark than in twenty-one basketball courts.

mountains seeking shelter from the fury of the storm. Some of the wicked people remembered Noah's ark. They pounded on the door and shouted "Let us in!" But it could not be opened. They were too late!

Forty days and nights it rained. The rising water lifted the ark from the place where Noah had built it, and the waves rocked it back and forth. The water rose higher and higher until the trees, rocks, and hills were covered. Men and women climbed the tallest mountains, but they could not find a way of escape from the rising waters.

The Flood covered all of the land and was at least twenty feet deep above the highest mountain. Every human being and all the animals were destroyed except those that were safe in the big ark.

THOUGHT QUESTION:

What was the first thing Noah and his family did after leaving the ark?

The Flood tore up the surface of the earth. Great rocks tumbled down from the mountains; forests were buried under tons of dirt, and many of the plants and animals were covered by sand and rocks. The trees and plants buried deep in the ground have since changed into black coal. In some of the layers of coal that are dug from mines today, you can find fern and leaf patterns showing that they originally came from the trees and vegetation before the Flood.

The mountains and valleys were never again as beautiful as when God created the earth. You can see scars and gashes made by the torrents of water on the sides of the mountains and through the valleys in many parts of the earth today. Researchers have dug up the shells of sea creatures on high mountains, showing that water once reached up to these high peaks.

During the storm, what happened to the ark? Noah and his family were safe in the boat, although it was pushed to and fro by the floodwaters. They must have longed for the winds and rain to stop, because the ark tossed and pitched on the stormy seas for five months! Finally the rain slowed and stopped, but the sturdy craft continued to float for several weeks.

While the boat was still drifting on the water, a day came when Noah decided to send out a raven. If there was dry land nearby, it would find a place to live. The bird flew back and forth but returned to the boat, and Noah knew that water still covered the earth.

A week later he let a dove fly from the ark, but she also returned. "Will the water always cover the earth?" the sons of Noah may have asked. But Noah remembered God's promise to save them all.

Another week passed, and Noah sent out the dove again. In the evening she returned with the leaf of an olive tree in her beak. Noah's family was very happy, because now they knew dry land had appeared and they could soon leave the ark.

A strong wind blew and began to dry the floodwaters, and the mountains appeared once more. The water dropped lower and lower until the boat finally settled on Mount Ararat. It was reassuring for Noah's family to feel something solid under their feet again!

Another week passed, and Noah let the dove fly away again. This time she did not come back. Then Noah took the cover off the top of the ark and looked out. There lay the dry surface of the earth.

"Go out of the ark, you and your wife, and your sons and your sons' wives with you," God said to Noah. "Bring out with you every living thing of all flesh that is with you: birds and cattle and every creeping thing that creeps on the earth, so that they may abound on the earth, and be fruitful and multiply on the earth."

Eight happy people left the boat that had been their home for many months. Now they could start a new life in a world that still kept much of its promise of beauty.

The first thing Noah did was to build an altar and offer a sacrifice to God for His love and His protection. The Lord had kept His promise,

Provonsha

and He blessed Noah and his family. God told them that He would never again destroy every living thing. And they would be protected from animals that were growing fierce and dangerous. From then on, the wild beasts and birds would be afraid of them.

As long as the world continued, the Lord said, there would be spring, summer, autumn, and winter. This was a blessing because people could expect the seasons to return at the regular time.

Days came when dark clouds gathered and rain fell on the earth. No doubt Noah and his sons wondered if there would be another flood, because they had not seen rainy weather in the world before the Flood. God wanted the people to feel safe, so He promised Noah that the world would never again be destroyed by water. As the sun shone through a shower of rain, Shem and Ham pointed to a great arch of many colors in the heavens above them. "What could that be?" they asked.

It was a rainbow. God said, "I set My rainbow in the cloud, and it shall be for the sign of the covenant between Me and the earth." The rainbow is a message from God which always reminds us that the earth will never again be destroyed by a flood of water. It is also a promise which someday God will make a new world like the perfect one He created in the beginning.

BUILDING THE FIRST CITY

Genesis 11

T he days were busy for Noah and his sons after they left the ark. They were happy to work, building homes, plowing fields, planting grain, and making vineyards, since they had been in the boat a long time without much to do. Within a few years, children and young people in Noah's sons' families had grown up and could help to harvest the crops and care for the herds of cows and flocks of sheep and goats.

Noah was 600 years old when he went into the ark, and he lived 350 years in the new world after the Flood. He told his grandchildren the story of how God saved them from the Flood. He repeated the promise of the coming Savior whom God would send to rescue people from sin and death forever.

Noah's children and grandchildren made their homes in the hills near the spot where the ark came to rest. As families increased in size, they moved down to the valleys and plains.

Some of the great-grandsons of Noah did not love God. They forgot how the Creator had brought their family safely through the terrible destruction of the Flood. They were only interested in wealth and property and in becoming powerful leaders. These men moved to the grassy plain called the land of Shinar. On this plain many families gathered, and they began to build the first cities.

Nimrod, a grandson of Ham, was one of the leaders. "He was a mighty hunter," the Bible says, and he established four cities. One of them, which later came to be called Babel, grew into a large city.

In that city, excitement rose among the people as word spread of the city leaders' plans.

"Did you hear?" said one storekeeper to a customer. "The leaders are going to build a gigantic tower that will reach to heaven."

"It can't be done," the customer answered.

"But the plans are already made," the excited store owner replied. "I heard a city leader say, 'Let's build a city and a tower for ourselves, whose top will reach high into the sky. We will become famous. Then we will not be scattered over all the earth.'"

Yes, the people had decided to build a great tower that would be the talk of the whole world. It would reach up toward the heavens, and if another flood came, they would climb to the top of the tower and be safe. The leaders of that large city had forgotten about God.

The people made bricks of clay and baked them in ovens until they were hard. Workers hauled them to the place where the foundations were laid. The people worked long hours, and the tower began to rise up from the ground. The city leaders were very proud! They were building a tower that would make their city famous.

One day while the leaders were giving commands for workers to carry brick and to mix mortar, a mysterious thing happened. The men could not understand the words the leaders were speaking. They were strange new sounds!

GOD SAYS:

"But the Lord came down to see the city and the tower which the sons of men had built." –Genesis 11:5

Up to this time "the whole earth had [only] one language." But now, the bricklayers seemed to be babbling as they waved their hands. The men who shouted orders to the stonecutters spoke a strange language, and the leaders were calling out in sounds none of the others could understand. It was as if people speaking Russian and Chinese and Spanish and English and Dutch were all trying to talk to each other in their own language.

What had happened? The people were proud and had forgotten God. They thought they could make the world perfect and safe by their own wisdom and strength. So the Creator God, who had made men and women in the first place and had given them the power to speak, created many languages for the people. Now they could not understand each others' words.

Work stopped immediately on the tower. Everyone was confused. Some of the leaders were angry, but what could they do? They shouted and clapped their hands,

QUICK FACT:

God did not want the people to live together in big cities. He wanted them to spread out into the countryside.

but the workers only shook their heads and then went home. There, the people of one family could not make out what their neighbors were saying.

Soon men and women began to move out of the city. If they could not tell the storekeepers what they wanted to buy, they would go and live somewhere else.

Groups of people who spoke the same language gathered together with all their possessions and left the city. Soon they had traveled far away. In this way the people were scattered from the wicked city, and the tower was never finished. The city became known as Babel, which sounds like the Hebrew word for confusion.

God had a purpose in scattering people all over the earth. They would be happier and have more to eat and more room if they lived in the country. When they refused to obey God's plan, He gave them many different languages, and then they could not live happily when they were crowded together in cities.

THOUGHT QUESTION:

Would the Tower of Babel have really saved the people from another flood?

The people of Babel thought that God could not see what they were doing when they tried to build the tower. They said they would do whatever they pleased; it was their business, and nobody could stop them. But God looked down from heaven and saw the wickedness in their thoughts, words, and actions. In a moment of time He changed all their plans because they refused to love and trust and obey Him.

God sees you and me. He looks at us with great love, and we love Him. We are willing to follow His ways because they are the best ways. He also knows about our mean thoughts and hateful actions, unkind or impure words, and knows if we cheat or steal or lie. When we give in to temptation, our heavenly Father fills us with sadness about it, and we will be sorry and turn away from doing wrong.

When we confess our sins to Him, God will forgive them and help us through His Holy Spirit to reject bad words, selfish thoughts, and impure actions. That way God makes us into His loving children, ready for heaven!

A BRAVE TRAVELER

Genesis 11; 12

One of the oldest cities mentioned in the Bible is a place called Ur of the Chaldees. It was situated near the river Euphrates in the land now called Iraq. Much of the city was built with strong baked bricks, and some of the city walls are still standing today.

In ancient times the people of Ur made idols and worshiped in temples of the moon-god. They also worshiped the sun. Besides making idols, the skilled workers of that city made beautiful gold objects, including cups and plates, weapons of war, and intricate jewelry.

We know about life in Ur because the people developed a way of writing on clay tablets. While the clay was still soft, they made wedge-shaped signs that we call *cuneiform.* Then the clay would harden, and the writing on the tablet became a permanent record.

In recent times, archaeologists have dug up many of the clay tablets on which are written such things as business deals like the buying of land and receipts for groceries. On one set of tablets, scientists discovered a complete but rather different version of the story of the Bible Flood.

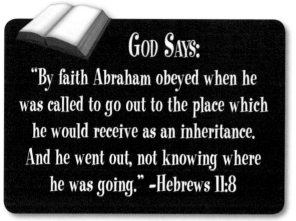

GOD SAYS:

"By faith Abraham obeyed when he was called to go out to the place which he would receive as an inheritance. And he went out, not knowing where he was going." –Hebrews 11:8

During those ancient times, one man who lived near Ur was named Terah. He was a descendant of Shem, the son of Noah. Terah was probably a farmer who kept cattle and sheep. His three sons were named Abram, Nahor, and Haran. The boys must have learned from their father how to take care of the flocks and herds.

The three sons grew up and got married. Haran and his wife had a son named Lot. Sometime later, Haran died, leaving Lot with a grandfather and uncles and aunts but no father. Nahor took a woman named Milcah to be his wife, and Abram married a woman named Sarai.

Terah may have worshiped in the temple of the moon-god. However, his son Abram had heard of the one true God, who created the earth and everything in it. Abram refused to worship any idols of wood or stone. The Lord God loved this faithful man and wanted to protect him and his family from the evil ways of the people around him. He commanded Abram to leave the city of Ur and move far away to the land called Canaan.

Terah and his grandson Lot started out on the journey toward Canaan with Abram and Sarai. They put their belongings on the backs of camels and donkeys and into four-wheeled carts. Terah and Abram directed the servants to gather the flocks of sheep and herds of cows together. Moving slowly, Terah's large family left Ur, the city they had known all their lives.

The caravan of people and animals traveled along the river valleys for about three hundred miles to the northwest. When they came to a town called Haran, old father Terah was ready to settle there for a while. Abram and the rest of the family stayed with him. As they raised animals and traded them, the wealth of the family grew. Terah lived to be 205 years old, and then he died.

> Abram remembered that God had said to him,
> "Get out of your country,
> From your [family]
> And from your father's house,
> To a land that I will show you.
> I will make you a great nation" (Genesis 12:1, 2).

With his father gone, Abram was now the leader of the family. He made plans to move on to Canaan as God had instructed him.

One morning the servants received orders to load the pack

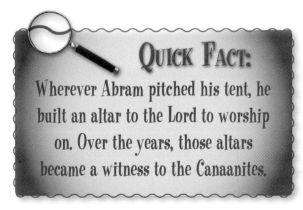

QUICK FACT: Wherever Abram pitched his tent, he built an altar to the Lord to worship on. Over the years, those altars became a witness to the Canaanites.

animals and get the carts ready for the journey. When all was ready, Abram gave the signal to start, and the caravan moved out of Haran. It must have been a long parade of camels, donkeys, carts, sheep, and cattle that began moving toward the southwest from Haran.

On this dangerous journey, the caravan would have to cross the hot desert of Syria. Water was scarce in that sandy country. Sometimes, when caravans lost their way, people and animals died of thirst. Then, too, thieves were hiding in some places along the roads, waiting among the rocks to attack travelers and rob them of their possessions. But God protected the caravan of Abram as it moved toward the land of Canaan.

After weeks, and perhaps months, of tiresome travel, the large group arrived in the area of Shechem. There Abram found a grove of oak trees and a wide grassy valley—an ideal place to pitch his

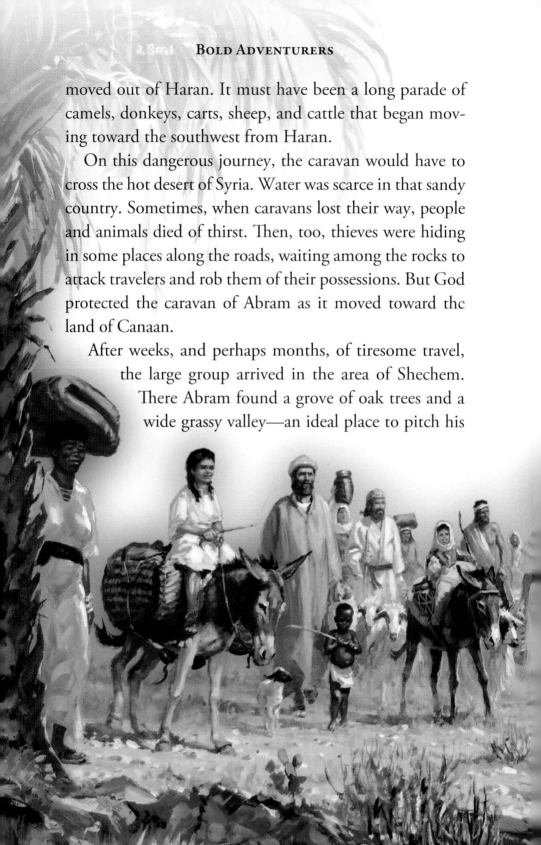

tents. He was thankful God had protected his family, his servants, and his herds of animals. He built an altar at Shechem and offered a Thank-You offering to the Lord.

As Abram traveled through that land, he saw streams of water tumbling over the rocks and through the valleys. He saw fields of wheat and barley, grapevines, fig trees, and olive groves.

The Lord said to Abram, "To your descendents I will give this land." But it seemed like a strange promise to Abram, for he was more than seventy-five years old, and he and Sarai had no children.

It took a lot of courage for Abram to believe that God would give him this land,
because the people
living

there were fierce fighters, and they did not welcome a stranger kindly. But Abram, "the friend of God," talked with the Lord one night under the starry sky, and God repeated the promise that he would be the father of a great nation.

Soon a day came when Abram commanded his servants to load the donkeys and the carts once more. Abram and Lot had decided to move south again. This time they came near the town of Bethel and pitched their tents. Abram built another altar to the God of heaven and prayed to Him.

THOUGHT QUESTION:

Why was Abram called "the friend of God"?

While Abram and Lot lived near Bethel, a year came when no rain fell. The rivers grew shallow and finally dried up. With worried looks, the herdsmen came to Abram to tell him that the grass was dead and almost gone, and there was little for the sheep and cattle to eat. What should they do to save the flocks and herds from starving? The servants wondered if Abram would leave this land when trouble came to him.

Sometimes Abram thought of the old home far off in the land of Ur, but his courage and faith did not fail in this crisis. He decided to take his family to Egypt, where there was plenty of food. They could live in that country on the rich meadowland watered by the Nile River. They would stay only until the rains returned to the land of Canaan and made it green again.

A SELFISH CHOICE AND A KIDNAPPING

Genesis 13–16

When he arrived in Egypt, Abram met Pharaoh, as the king was called, and received gifts from him. But when the famine had ended, the brave traveler was anxious to return to Canaan. The caravan traveled back to Bethel, where Abram and Lot again pitched their tents.

By this time Abram was very rich in cattle and in silver and gold. Lot also had many flocks and herds. The animals needed plenty of pasture, and the servants of Abram began to quarrel with the servants of Lot over the best grazing land.

When Abram heard of the trouble, he said to his nephew, Lot, "Please let there be no strife between you and me, and between my herdsmen and your herdsmen; for we are brethren" (Genesis 13:8).

Abram loved peace and was an unselfish man. Even though he was older than Lot and should have taken first choice of the pasture land, he offered the younger man any part of the country he wanted. Lot looked over the land around them and picked the rich plain of the Jordan River valley.

Lot made a sad mistake when he moved to this valley. If he had talked the matter over with his uncle, Abram

would no doubt have told him not to go there because of the sinful people living nearby. But Lot was selfish and thought only about how rich he could become, and this caused him to overlook the dangers in that part of the land.

In this valley were two cities called Sodom and Gomorrah. They were known for their crime and wickedness; but Lot did not think about this. He took his wife and children, his servants, his sheep, his camels, and his gold, and set up his tents near Sodom.

God Says:
"Let each of you look out not only for his own interests, but also for the interests of others." –Philippians 2:4

Abram moved to the hills of Hebron, south of Bethel, and pitched his tents under the shady oak trees there. He was now a chief in that land, and people knew him to be an honest, unselfish man. Faithful and true to God, Abram was blessed with riches, and he was at peace with all the people around him.

One day a stranger rode furiously into the camp of Abram. Not stopping to catch his breath, the man told how he had just escaped from the armies of four kings who had taken him prisoner. The soldiers of these kings had been fighting in the Jordan valley, and they had kidnapped all the men and women from the cities of Sodom and Gomorrah. Lot and his family and all that he owned had been captured by the enemy, and the soldiers were carrying them away as prisoners. Lot's selfishness had brought him into serious trouble.

Abram quickly called 318 of his servants who were trained warriors, and together they set out after the armies of the four kings. He was hoping to save Lot and his family. Across the plains and over the hills, Abram rode at the head of the troop.

Could this band of men fight the armies of the enemy kings and rescue the prisoners? Abram must have thought about this many times. He knew they faced serious dangers, but he was not afraid, because he trusted God.

Day after day Abram and his men pursued the armies. It was not difficult to follow the trail. But would they be able to save Lot and his family when they caught up with the enemy? Often these fierce kings tortured and killed their prisoners. Although the nephew had been selfish in his dealings with his uncle, Abram did not think about it. He loved Lot and wanted to save him and his family from a terrible fate.

One night, a couple of Abram's men who were scouting ahead of the troop, came upon the enemy. They discovered the camp near the town of Dan. The armies had settled down for the night, and the guards were sleepy. Abram divided his troop of warriors into groups, and they surrounded the camp.

At the signal to attack, those valiant men rushed forward and surprised the enemy

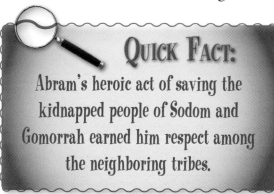

QUICK FACT:
Abram's heroic act of saving the kidnapped people of Sodom and Gomorrah earned him respect among the neighboring tribes.

guards. The king of Elam was killed, and the armies fled. Abram's men chased the soldiers until they reached the town of Hobah. Lot and his family, as well as many other prisoners, were set free, and all of their possessions were saved. Abram and Lot had a happy reunion, and soon they started a victory march toward home.

THOUGHT QUESTION:
What promises did God make to Abram after he rescued Lot?

The king of Sodom heard the news, and he rode out to meet Abram's troop of warriors. Grateful that his people had been rescued, the king offered to let Abram keep all the treasure he had captured from the four kings. "Take the goods for yourself," the king urged.

"I will take nothing, from a thread to a sandal strap," Abram said to the king. "I will not take anything that is yours, lest you should say, 'I have made Abram rich.'"

On the homeward journey Abram met a priest of God named Melchizedek. This good priest blessed the brave leader, and Abram gave the priest a tenth of all the goods he had taken. The Lord instructs us to give Him a tenth, or tithe, of what we earn. We happily give a tenth to our Creator for the life and health that He gives us. Abram gave God a tenth, and he was blessed. Truly Abram loved the Lord with all his heart, and he was the friend of God.

One evening soon after the rescue of Lot, Abram was walking in the cool night air. He was troubled as he thought of the enemy kings, and how they might return and attack him and his family. He knew they were cruel warriors who would try to get revenge if they could.

While he was considering this danger, God said: "Do not be

afraid, Abram. I am your shield, your exceedingly great reward." The man gained courage and believed that he would be protected. He also remembered that God had said all the land of Canaan would be given to his family.

Abram was almost ninety years old now, and he had no children. He wondered how his family could possess all the land from Egypt north to the Euphrates—a land almost five hundred miles long—if he had no sons or daughters. God said to him, "Look now toward heaven, and count the stars if you are able to number them." And He said to him, "So shall your descendants be."

While the Lord talked with Abram, He also told him that someday his descendants would go to a strange land where they would be slaves for hundreds of years; but the time would come when they would return to their own country of Canaan.

When Abram was ninety-nine years old, the Lord told him he should have a new name. "No longer shall your name be called Abram, but your name shall be Abraham; for I have made you a father of many nations." The name Abram meant an "honored father," while Abraham was a name with greater significance, meaning, "father of a multitude." His wife Sarai's name was changed to Sarah, which means "the princess of the multitude."

VISITORS ON A STRANGE MISSION

Genesis 18; 19

O ne day about noon Abraham was sitting in the door-
way of his tent. He saw three strangers coming up
the road, and they looked tired and dusty. Abraham was
always ready to welcome visitors, so he hurried out to meet
the men.

He bowed to them and said, "My Lord, if I have now
found favor in Your sight, do not pass on by Your servant.
Please let a little water be brought, and wash your feet, and
rest yourselves under the tree. And I will bring a morsel of
bread, that you may refresh your hearts. After that you
may pass by, inasmuch as you have come to your servant."

"Do as you have said," they replied, accepting the kindness of their host.

According to the custom of that country, Abraham
brought a basin of water, and the men removed their san-
dals and washed their feet. Abraham hurried back to the
tent and asked Sarah to bake barley cakes. Then he went

to the field and chose a calf from his herd, slaughtered it, and gave it to a servant to prepare for the men to eat. He had other servants bring butter and milk. The meal was served to the men as they sat in the shade of a large oak tree.

As Abraham talked with the strangers, he discovered that he was entertaining visitors from heaven. The Lord Himself and two of His angels had received a proper welcome from this hospitable man. No wonder Abraham was called "the friend of God."

After the travelers had eaten, they stood up and started on the road toward Sodom. Abraham walked with them a short distance to see them safely on their journey.

"Shall I hide from Abraham what I am doing," the Lord said, "since Abraham shall surely become a great and mighty nation?" No, the Lord would make His plans known to His faithful pioneer.

So what startling news was Abraham about to hear? He listened anxiously. "Because the outcry against Sodom and Gomorrah is great, and because their sin is very grievous," the Lord said to him, "I will go down now and see whether they have done altogether according to the outcry against it that has come to Me; and if not, I will know."

Abraham was worried when he heard this. He knew the cities were very wicked,

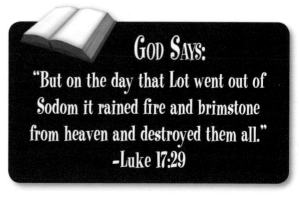

GOD SAYS:
"But on the day that Lot went out of Sodom it rained fire and brimstone from heaven and destroyed them all."
-Luke 17:29

He thought of Lot and his family who had moved to Sodom.

Two of the visitors hurried on toward the city, but the Lord remained to talk with His friend. Abraham came close to Him and said, "Would You . . . destroy the righteous with the wicked? Suppose there were fifty righteous within the city; would You . . . destroy the place and not spare it for the fifty righteous that were in it?"

So the Lord replied, "If I find in Sodom fifty righteous within the city, then I will spare . . . the place for their sakes."

Then Abraham thought for a moment. How many good people did he know in Sodom? Lot was a good man, but how many others were there? He was afraid there were not even fifty. Abraham asked if the Lord would save the cities if only forty-five good people could be found. The Lord agreed to this request.

But Abraham did not stop there. He persisted in trying to save those cities. Would God spare them if there were forty good men? Yes, was the reply. How about thirty? Yes was again the answer. If there were only ten good people? Once more the Lord agreed, saying, "I will not destroy [the city] for the sake of ten."

Abraham knew how to talk with his Creator. Many times under the stars of the night sky the man had prayed for faith and courage. Now he could plead with the Lord to spare these wicked cities if only ten good people lived in them, and the Lord agreed to his request. When the Lord had finished speaking, He told His friend goodbye and went on His way, and Abraham returned to his tents.

That evening the two angels arrived at the gates of the city of Sodom. Lot was one of the city leaders, and it was the custom for them to sit at the gate to help settle disputes and to act as judges.

On this afternoon Lot was sitting at the gate, ready to offer hospitality to strangers. In his polite manner, Lot welcomed the two visitors and urged them to go home with him for the night. They accepted Lot's invitation. He prepared a feast for them, and they ate very well.

The wicked men of Sodom heard that strangers had arrived in town, and they surrounded Lot's home. The mob planned to hurt the visitors if they could lay hands on

them. They began beating on the door of the house, and it looked as though Lot and his visitors were in serious trouble. But the angels struck the mob of men with blindness, and then they could do no harm.

When Lot saw what had happened, he realized that his guests were angels. Then the visitors gave him their message. This would be the last night for the men and women of Sodom, the angels told him. "The outcry against them has grown great before the face of the Lord," they said, "and the Lord has sent us to destroy it."

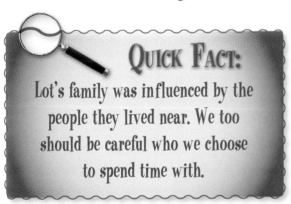

QUICK FACT:

Lot's family was influenced by the people they lived near. We too should be careful who we choose to spend time with.

Lot hurried out to warn his married daughters, but their husbands laughed at him when he said the city would be burned up. They thought he was joking, because they did not think anything could happen to their proud city.

No, there were not fifty in Sodom who loved God and believed His word. There were not twenty or even ten such faithful people. The Lord could not spare that wicked city. But He did save those who were willing to obey His instructions.

Lot must have talked a long time with his wife and his two unmarried daughters that night, telling them about the terrible fate that awaited Sodom. Early the next morning the angels urged Lot to get out of the city. "Arise, take your wife and your two daughters who are here," said the guests, "lest you be consumed in the punishment of the city."

But it was hard for them to say goodbye to their home. Lot thought of his wealth, and his wife remembered her friends. The husband and wife stood at the door of the house and didn't move.

Finally the angels could wait no longer. In the early morning darkness, they took Lot's wife and his daughters by the hand and led them to the gates of Sodom. "Escape for your life!" cried the angels. "Do not look behind you nor stay anywhere in the plain. Escape to the mountains, lest you be destroyed." There was no time to stop and think about it.

The frightened family hurried along the road leading out of the valley. *"Don't look back, don't look back!"* The words went through their minds over and over. But Lot's heart was still in Sodom, and his wife remembered her friends and her relatives. The daughters thought of the parties and good times they had enjoyed. *"Don't look back!"* Again the words prompted them to keep going.

Thought Question:
Why did Lot's wife turn into a pillar of salt?

But then Lot's wife hesitated. She had to look back! Besides, it was foolish for them to hurry and leave, she thought. Instead of being thankful, she was angry. She would turn around and see if anything was happening to Sodom. She refused to obey God's instruction.

As she turned and looked back, something dreadful happened. She turned into a pillar of salt. What a strange monument to disobedience! There in the valley by the roadside stood a statue of salt that had been Lot's wife, a fearful symbol of what it costs to disobey the Lord's commands.

Lot and his two daughters hurried on to the small city of Zoar. As the morning sunshine came over the hills, they entered the gates of the town.

And what was happening back in Sodom? People began to go about the streets as usual that morning. Men opened businesses in the markets where they bought and sold their goods. The sons-in-law of Lot who had refused to go with him laughed as they thought of the man and his family hurrying away from the city.

Suddenly out of the clear sky came an explosion of fire! Sulphur and flames fell on Sodom and Gomorrah. The palaces and temples, the crowds of wicked people, the homes and gardens—all were destroyed! Smoke rolled up into the sky as if a giant furnace were blazing.

Abraham got up early that morning and looked down the road toward Sodom. He was anxious to know if the Lord had found ten good men in Sodom and Gomorrah. Then he saw the smoke! It rose higher and higher in big black clouds. The cities were being destroyed.

Later Abraham found out that the angels had been able to save only Lot and his wife and their two unmarried daughters from the wicked cities of the Jordan Valley, and even Lot's wife had come to a tragic end because she disobeyed.

ABRAHAM'S TWO SONS

Genesis 16; 21

Abraham and Sarah trusted in God, but since they had no children they often wondered how it would be possible for their descendants to own the land of Canaan. One day Sarah suggested to her husband that he should follow the custom of some of the people and marry a second wife. If the second wife had children, Abraham would be able to pass on to them the land God had promised him.

Sarah told her husband Abraham that her maid, Hagar, would be a good wife. Hagar was an Egyptian woman who had been with Abraham's family for the ten years since they left Egypt. She had learned to love and worship the true God.

So, Abraham accepted Sarah's plan and married Hagar. But two wives in the home did not bring happiness. Hagar and Sarah quarreled, and one day the maid was so unhappy that she ran away into the desert.

Where shall I go? What shall I do? These were the questions that worried Hagar as she stumbled along the hot, dusty trail. She wanted to go back to Egypt, but it was a long way to travel across the desert. Finally she found a fountain of water by the side of the trail, and here she stopped to rest. An angel came to her and said, "Hagar, Sarai's maid, where have you come from, and where are you going?"

"I am fleeing from the presence of my mistress Sarai," was all the maid could say, because she did not know where she was going. Then the angel told her she should go back to Abraham's home. Hagar obeyed the angel and returned to her work of serving Sarah; but life was not pleasant for her.

After a time Hagar and Abraham had a son, and they named him Ishmael. Now

> **QUICK FACT:**
> Abraham believed in God's promise, but he didn't wait for God to fulfill it in His own time and way. This brought trouble and pain to Abraham's home.

Abraham was happy, because he thought he could see how his descendants might someday possess the Promised Land.

The boy Ishmael grew to be a strong teenager, and he loved to shoot with the bow and arrow. When he was fourteen years old, and Abraham and his family were living at a place called Gerar, not far from the land of Egypt, Abraham's wife Sarah had a baby. This was the son that God had long ago promised to Sarah and Abraham. They named the baby Isaac, which means laughter, and the father, who was now one hundred years old, took great pride in his baby son.

When Isaac grew older, he played with Ishmael. Abraham made a feast for Isaac when he was old enough to walk. It must have been a happy day for friends and neighbors who came to celebrate with the parents. But the happiness was spoiled, because Ishmael teased young Isaac. This made Sarah very angry. She went to Abraham and demanded that Ishmael and his mother, Hagar, be sent away from their home.

What was Abraham to do? He loved his son Ishmael, and he did not want to send Hagar away. But there would be no peace in his tents while there was hatred between Hagar and Sarah.

So Abraham prayed, and the Lord told him that it was best for Ishmael and his mother to leave. Then the Lord said, "As for Ishmael, . . . I have blessed him, and will make him fruitful, and will multiply him exceedingly. . . . I will make him a great nation. But My covenant I will establish with Isaac" (Genesis 17:20).

Early the next morning, Abraham called Hagar and told her she must take her son and leave his home. He gave her some food and an animal skin filled with water. Abraham told Ishmael and Hagar goodbye, and with sadness in his heart he watched the mother and son start off on the road that led into the desert of Beersheba.

Hagar trudged along the rough road, and after a while she realized that she was lost. The animal-skin canteen of water was empty, and the hot sun of the desert beat down on them. Ishmael grew thirsty and tired. At last he could go no farther, so his mother laid him under a bush and went and sat down a little way off. "Let me not see the death of the boy!" she cried.

God was watching over them, and soon an angel came to her. "What ails you, Hagar? Fear not, for God has heard the voice of the lad where he is. Arise, lift up the lad and hold him with your hand, for I will make him a great nation."

The woman brushed the tears from her eyes and looked around her. Then she stood up and looked again. What did she see? Not far away was a well of water! She ran to the well, filled the animal skin, and carried it to her son.

And so Ishmael and his mother were able to continue on their journey. They made their home in the desert, and Ishmael grew to be a strong man, skillful in hunting with the bow and arrow.

THOUGHT QUESTION:

Why did Ishmael have to leave?

Ishmael married a woman from Egypt, and his twelve sons were warriors in the desert. They lived in tents and moved from place to place with their flocks. Their descendants live in the desert country to this day.

ABRAHAM'S GREATEST TEST

Genesis 22

If you have a friend who always keeps her word, you know she can be depended on when you are in trouble. Abraham had found God to be such a friend. You remember that the pioneer left his home in Ur and traveled to a strange country when God called him to go. Abraham had met famine and war along the way, but the Lord protected His friend in times of danger.

Abraham had been greatly blessed, and now he was living at Beersheba, where thousands of his sheep fed on the grass-covered hills, and hundreds of servants and their families lived in tents. Remember, too, that Abraham followed the Lord's instructions when there was trouble in his home. Although he was sorry to send Hagar and Ishmael away, he believed God knew best.

Abraham had lived more than a hundred years, and now his greatest happiness was in being with his son Isaac, who had grown to be a healthy young man. Abraham depended on Isaac to help run the business and to deal with

the servants. The father knew that if the son was to possess the land of Canaan as God had said, he must become a strong, dependable leader.

One night while the pioneer stood watching the stars, the Lord spoke to him again. "Abraham!" He said.

"Here I am," said Abraham.

"Take now your son," said the Lord, "your only son Isaac, whom you love, and go to the land of Moriah, and offer him there as a burnt offering on one of the mountains of which I shall tell you."

Abraham had trusted God through all his life, and surely He would not fail him now. But why would the Lord ask him to do such a terrible thing? Wasn't Isaac the son that was to inherit the promised country of Canaan? If he was killed, how would Abraham's family ever possess that beautiful land?

Early in the morning Abraham awakened Isaac and two of his servants and told them they were going on a trip with him to offer sacrifices. Isaac had often gone with his father to worship God, so he was not surprised to be called for such a journey. The servants chopped wood, tied it in bundles, and placed it on a donkey. With no matches or lighters in those days, they probably had to carry hot coals of fire in a pot.

The father and son set out on their journey to the land of Moriah, the place where the city of Jerusalem would someday be built. They did not awaken Sarah to tell her goodbye, because Abraham was afraid if he told his wife the sad news, she would stop him from obeying God.

The land of Moriah was about fifty miles from their home in Beersheba, and it was not until the morning of the third day of travel that Abraham saw the mountain where he was to make the sacrifice. When they came to the foot of the mountain, Abraham told his servants to stay there with the donkey. Pointing to the mountaintop, the father said, "The lad and I will go yonder and worship, and we will come back to you."

The servants waited with the pack animal, and the father and son began climbing the mountain together. Isaac carried the heavy bundle of wood, while his father carried the knife and the fire.

Noticing that they had no lamb to offer on the altar, Isaac stopped. He thought his father had forgotten to bring a sacrifice. "My father!" Isaac said to Abraham.

"Here I am, my son," Abraham responded.

"Look, the fire and the wood," he said, "but where is the lamb for a burnt offering?"

"My son, God will provide for Himself the lamb for a burnt offering," Abraham said. Then the father and the son continued their climb. Abraham did not have the heart to tell Isaac that he was to be the sacrifice until it was absolutely necessary.

Finally the two came to the place where God had directed that the altar was to be built. They gathered stones and piled them to make the altar and then arranged the wood carefully on

GOD SAYS:

"Take now your son, your only son Isaac, whom you love, and go to the land of Moriah, and offer him there as a burnt offering on one of the mountains." –Genesis 22:2

the stones. When there was nothing more to prepare, Abraham told Isaac about God's command.

The young man listened to his father and was willing to obey and to be the sacrifice. He could easily have

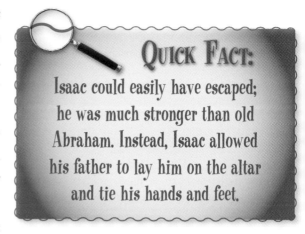

QUICK FACT:

Isaac could easily have escaped; he was much stronger than old Abraham. Instead, Isaac allowed his father to lay him on the altar and tie his hands and feet.

run away if he wanted to, but he allowed his father to lay him on the altar and to tie his hands and feet.

The hour of greatest test had come to Abraham. He knew that the people who worshiped the sun-god in the land of Ur sometimes offered their children as sacrifices to idols, but the true God had never made such a terrible request before. In this moment, Abraham did not disobey God. He lifted the knife to kill his son.

As he raised his hand ready to strike, a Voice called from heaven: "Abraham! Abraham!"

"Here I am," he replied.

"Do not lay your hand on the lad," the Voice said, "or do anything to him; for now I know that you fear God, seeing you have not withheld your son, your only son, from Me."

Abraham could have shouted for joy. His son was safe! His love and loyalty to God had been severely tested, but he had proved true.

Then Abraham saw in the bushes a ram caught by its horns. So he grabbed the animal and offered it as a sacrifice to the Lord. He named that place Jehovah-jireh, which

THOUGHT QUESTION:

Why did God tell Abraham to kill his own son?

means "The Lord will provide."

A very happy father and son hiked down the mountain together and met the waiting servants. Soon they were on their way home to Beersheba. Young Isaac must have realized as never before that God had special work for him to do, because his life had been wonderfully spared.

THE SEARCH FOR A BRIDE

Genesis 23–25:9

Abraham moved his family, his flocks, and his herds once more. He left Beersheba to return to Hebron, where the oak trees had given cooling shade for his tents many years earlier. It was near Hebron that Abraham was living at the time he and Lot went separate ways. There the Lord and two angels had visited the faithful pioneer; and there, too, Isaac had been born. Abraham was returning to a place of happy memories.

Soon after the return, Sarah died, and Abraham wept over losing her. As a loyal wife, she had gone with him to Egypt in time of famine; she had stood with her husband before kings and princes. She had been the mother of Isaac, as God had promised. And now, at the age of 127 years, she passed to her rest.

Abraham wished to bury his wife in the Cave of Machpelah, which was near Hebron, so he went to Ephron the Hittite, the owner of the land where the cave was located, and bought the field. When the purchase was completed,

Abraham buried his wife in the cave.

As the years passed, this faithful friend of God grew old and weak. He gave all his property to Isaac and asked him to take charge of the cattle,

the sheep, and the other possessions. The son was now forty years of age, but he had never married. Abraham had warned his son that the people of Canaan worshiped idols, and he told Isaac he should not marry a daughter of the neighboring families.

But where was Isaac to find a wife? This was a concern to Abraham, because he wished to see his son have a home of his own and children who would possess the great country God had promised them.

One day Abraham thought of a plan to get a wife for Isaac. He called his oldest and most trusted servant, Eliezer, and gave him an important mission. He said, "You shall go to my country and to my [family], and take a wife for my son Isaac."

"Perhaps the woman will not be willing to follow me to this land. Must I take your son back to the land from which you came?"

Abraham told Eliezer that Isaac must not go back to the country he had come from. His son might be tempted to stay there among idol worshipers. He said to Eliezer, "Beware that you do not take my son back there. The Lord

God of heaven, who took me from my father's house and from the land of my [family], and who spoke to me and swore to me, saying, 'To your descendants I give this land,' He will send His angel before you, and you shall take a wife for my son from there."

If the woman Eliezer chose to be Isaac's wife was unwilling to come back with him, then the servant was released from his special duty. "Only do not take my son back there," the father warned again.

The servants prepared ten camels for the caravan. The animals were roped together, one behind another, to form a line. Tied to their harness were bronze bells that tinkled as the camels moved. The servants also filled sacks with food. Then Eliezer placed valuable gifts in some strong leather bags—presents for the girl he would find. The camels were made to kneel and the bags loaded on their backs.

When the camel train was ready, Eliezer gave the signal to his fellow servants, and they started the camels forward on the road leading northward toward the land of Mesopotamia.

Days and weeks passed as they walked through the desert, until the caravan arrived one afternoon at the gates of the city of Haran. Eliezer made the camels kneel beside the town well, where the women came to draw water in the evening. The hour of the test had come. How would this servant know which of the young women he should choose?

Eliezer believed in the Lord God, and he prayed for help. "O Lord God of my master Abraham," he said,

"please give me success this day, and show kindness to my master Abraham. Behold, I stand here by the well of water, and the daughters of the men of the city are coming out to draw water. Now let it be that the young woman to whom I say, 'Please let down your pitcher that I may drink,' and she says, 'Drink, and I will also give your camels a drink'—let her be the one whom You have appointed for Your servant Isaac. And by this I will know that You have shown kindness to my master."

Before he had finished his prayer, a beautiful young woman came to the well carrying a clay pitcher on her shoulder. She stepped down to the fountain, filled her pitcher, and was coming up the steps when Eliezer ran to her and said, "Please let me drink a little water from your pitcher."

"Drink, [sir]," she said, and quickly lowering the pitcher from her shoulder, she gave him a drink. Then she said, "I will draw water for your camels, also, until they have finished drinking." When camels are thirsty, they can drink up to thirty-two gallons of water, and the girl must have carried her pitcher many times from the well to the watering trough.

While the young woman was doing this good deed, Eliezer looked on in silence. He saw his prayer being answered before his eyes! When the camels had finished drinking, the man took a gold nose ring and two golden bracelets from his bag of gifts and gave them to the girl. Then he asked, "Whose daughter are you? Tell me, please, is there room in your father's house for us to lodge?"

The young woman told him her name was Rebekah and that she was the daughter of Bethuel, the son of Nahor, Abraham's brother. "We have both straw and feed enough," she added, "and room to lodge."

Then the servant thanked God for answering his prayer. The girl ran home and told her mother about the guest who had given her beautiful gifts of gold.

Rebekah's brother, Laban, saw the rich treasures, and he went quickly to the well and found Eliezer beside his camels. He welcomed the man. "Come in, O blessed of the Lord!" he said. "Why do you stand outside? For I have prepared the house, and a place for the camels."

After the camels had been unloaded and fed, Eliezer and his companions were given water to wash their feet, and food was set before them. But Eliezer pushed the food aside, saying, "I will not eat until I have told about my errand."

"Speak on," Laban said, anxious to know the man's business.

Abraham's servant began by telling of his master's riches and of his son. Then he explained why he had been sent on this long journey. He was to find a bride for Isaac. When he said this, he must have looked at Rebekah, and the girl must have known what he meant. He told how he arrived at the city of Haran that afternoon, and how he had prayed that the woman who came to the well and offered him a drink of water, and who gave water to the camels, might be the one who should be the bride for Isaac.

While the family listened, Eliezer told how Rebekah

came to the well and gave him a drink of water from her pitcher and then gave water to his camels. The answer to his prayer had been so remarkable that Eliezer said, "I bowed my head and worshiped the Lord, and blessed the Lord God of my master Abraham, who had led me in the way of truth to take the daughter of my master's brother for his son. Now if you will deal kindly and truly with my master, tell me. And if not, tell me, that I may turn to the right hand or to the left."

The family was amazed at the story, and Laban and his father Bethuel answered, "The thing comes from the Lord; we cannot speak to you either bad or good. Here is Rebekah before you; take her and go, and let her be your master's son's wife, as the Lord has spoken."

When Abraham's servant heard these

QUICK FACT:

Choosing a wife for Isaac was very important to Abraham. He wanted Isaac to marry a girl who wouldn't lead him away from God.

words, he again thanked God for His blessings. Then he opened his bag of treasures and brought out gifts of silver and gold for Rebekah. He also gave her many beautiful garments. Then he gave presents to her mother and to her brother, Laban. When this was done, Eliezer and his men ate and drank, and they stayed at the home that night.

The next morning Eliezer awakened his companions, and they prepared the caravan for the journey back to Hebron. Eliezer was anxious to get started, so he said to Rebekah's mother and brother, "Send me away to my master."

But the family did not like to see Rebekah go away from home so soon. The mother thought of the time needed to get Rebekah's clothes ready for the journey and also for her wedding. So they said, "Let the young woman stay with us a few days, at least ten; after that she may go."

"Do not hinder me," he said to them, "since the Lord has prospered my way; send me away so that I may go to my master."

"We will call the young woman and ask her personally," they said. So they called Rebekah and said to her, "Will you go with this man?"

"I will go," she replied without hesitation.

Quickly the animals were loaded, and Rebekah said Goodbye to her family. The caravan started, and the girl and her maidservants rode away on the camels toward a new home and a husband she had never seen. Eliezer thanked God for answering his prayer and making his mission a success.

While all this was happening, Isaac was in the tents at Hebron. He had not forgotten that Eliezer had gone to find him a bride. Each day he thought of the caravan and wondered if his servant was having success in his mission.

One evening as the shadows grew long under the oak trees, Isaac went for a walk in the field. He was thinking of the bride who might be traveling to him, and he prayed that God would guide and bless her.

In the still evening air he heard the tinkle of bells and knew that a caravan was near. They sounded like the bells of his camels. Isaac looked across the field and saw the caravan coming toward him. Yes, they were his camels! Eliezer was coming home.

Now Rebekah saw a man hurrying across the field. She asked Eliezer, "Who is this man walking in the field to meet us?"

"It is my master," replied the servant.

The young woman stopped her camel, commanded it to kneel, and she dismounted.

She took a veil and covered herself, as was the custom of the country.

When Isaac came near, his servant told him all that had happened and how the Lord had blessed him in finding the girl. Then Eliezer presented Rebekah to his master.

As the crimson sunset lighted the sky, the girl and Isaac walked across the field together toward the tents of Abraham. Isaac heard Rebekah speak to him, and her words blended with the tinkle of the camel bells. In the soft evening light Isaac could see that his bride was beautiful, and he knew from the story Eliezer had told him that she was kind and thoughtful to others. He was thankful that Rebekah had been brave enough to come on the long journey to a strange land to be his wife.

THOUGHT QUESTION:

How did Eliezer know that Rebekah was the woman God had chosen to marry Isaac?

The couple was married, and Isaac loved his wife. He was no longer lonely as he had been after the death of his mother.

There were years of happiness for Abraham, and for Isaac and Rebekah. When Abraham was 175 years old, he died. The pioneer had been a friend of God all his life. Ishmael heard of his father's death, and he came from his desert home to attend the funeral. The two sons, Isaac and Ishmael, buried their father in the Cave of Machpelah, where Sarah had been laid to rest.

THE ADVENTURES OF TWIN BOYS

Genesis 25:24–34; 27–28:5

Twin boys were born to Isaac and Rebekah, and the parents named their sons Esau and Jacob. Esau, the older boy, grew up to be strong and bold. He liked to hike over the hills and through the valleys hunting for deer with his bow and arrows. He was a skillful hunter, and when he drew back his bow with his muscular, hairy arm, the arrow went straight to its mark.

Jacob, the younger son, was quite different from his brother. He was quiet and thoughtful, and he enjoyed watching the flocks and staying near his home.

Esau was the favorite of his father. Isaac greatly admired his son who roamed the country as an adventurous hunter. He also enjoyed the deer meat that Esau prepared as a tasty meal. Rebekah loved Jacob more, and she spoiled him until he came to think only of himself and of having his own way.

One day Esau came home from a hunting trip. He had walked miles and miles through the wild country without seeing a deer. He was so weak and hungry he thought he would die. When Esau came near the tents of his father, he saw Jacob cooking a stew of red lentils. The food smelled good!

"Please feed me with that same red stew, for I am weary," Esau said to his brother.

Jacob should have given his hungry brother some of the food at once, but instead he said to Esau, "Sell me your birthright as of this day."

The birthright was the special honor given to the eldest son of the family. He was given higher rank above his brothers and sisters, and usually his father left him the greater part of the lands, cattle, and money. The one with the birthright was specially blessed and dedicated to God, and it was his duty to care for the family when the father died.

Since Esau loved the carefree life of a hunter, he did not consider the birthright of much value. He said to his brother, "Look, I am about to die; so what profit shall this birthright be to me?" In this way Esau gave his birthright to his brother. Just to be sure, Jacob said, "Swear to me as of this day."

Esau swore to keep his promise, and then Jacob gave his brother a dish of bread and lentils. Esau ate quickly and went on his way. As Jacob saw his brother leave, he thought he had been clever to get this promise from his brother. But he had done wrong by this selfish trick.

Isaac moved his family and his tents from place to place over the years and finally settled at Beersheba, where his father Abraham had lived. When he was old, Isaac became blind. One day he called his favorite son to his tent. "My son!" he said to him.

"Here I am," Esau replied.

"Behold now, I am old," Isaac said. "I do not know the day of my death. Now therefore, please take your weapons, your quiver and your bow, and go out to the field and hunt game for me. And make me savory food, such as I love, and bring it to me that I may eat, that my soul may bless you before I die."

But someone else was at the door of the tent listening to Isaac's words. It was his wife, Rebekah, and she wanted Jacob to have the blessing. While Esau took his bow and arrows and started on his hunting trip, she began planning with Jacob. She told him to bring her two small goats from the flock. She cooked a dish of meat that smelled and tasted almost like the deer meat that Esau usually prepared.

Jacob was worried. He did not like to deceive his father, and he did not want to disobey his mother. What if the plan failed? He knew his father could not see him, but he was sure Isaac would feel his arms and his neck. Jacob was not hairy like Esau.

Rebekah had Jacob put on Esau's best clothes, and then she took pieces of goatskin and spread them over her son's arms and neck. She put the dish of hot food in his hands and sent him to Isaac.

When Jacob came near the old man, he said, "My father!"

"Here I am," Isaac replied. "Who are you, my son?"

Jacob said to his father, "I am Esau your firstborn; I have done just as you told me; please arise, sit and eat of my game, that your soul may bless me."

Isaac said to his son, "How is it that you have found it so quickly, my son?"

"Because the Lord your God brought it to me," he said.

But all that Jacob said to his father was a lie.

Then blind Isaac said, "Please come near, that I may feel you, my son, whether you are really my son Esau or not." So Jacob went up to his father Isaac, who put his hands on him and said, "The voice is Jacob's voice, but the hands are the hands of Esau." Isaac still wasn't sure who he was talking to.

THOUGHT QUESTION:

Why was having the birthright so important to Jacob?

"Are you really my son Esau?" he asked.

"I am," Jacob replied, telling another lie to his father. In this way the aged father was tricked by his son Jacob.

"Bring [the food] near to me, and I will eat of my son's game, so that my soul may bless you."

The old man ate the dish of good-tasting food and drank the wine Jacob gave him, and then he said, "Come near now and kiss me, my son." Jacob went to his father and kissed him. Isaac smelled his robes, and blessed him saying,

> "Surely, the smell of my son
> Is like the smell of a field
> Which the Lord has blessed.
> Therefore may God give you
> Of the dew of heaven,
> Of the fatness of the earth,
> And plenty of grain and wine.
> Let peoples serve you,
> And nations bow down to you.
> Be master over your brethren,
> And let your mother's sons bow down to you.
> Cursed be everyone who curses you,
> And blessed be those who bless you!" (Genesis 27:26–29).

Jacob had received the birthright blessing from his father, and he had cheated Esau. He hurried from his father's tent, because he was afraid of what might happen if his brother found him there.

A few minutes after Jacob left, Esau came back from hunting. He prepared the food that Isaac loved and

> **GOD SAYS:**
> "And the older shall serve the younger." –Genesis 25:23

brought it to his blind father. He said, "Let my father arise and eat of his son's game, that your soul may bless me."

"Who are you?" his father asked him.

"I am your son," he said, "your firstborn, Esau."

The old man began to tremble, because he knew something was wrong. "Who? Where is the one who hunted game and brought it to me? I ate all of it before you came, and I have blessed him—and indeed he shall be blessed."

Then the strong hunter cried loud and bitterly. He knew he had been tricked by his brother, Jacob. "Bless me, even me also, O my father!" he begged.

Isaac told his son that Jacob had stolen his richest blessing, and it could not be given to another. Esau thought
about his brother and said, "He took away my birthright,
and now look, he has taken away my blessing!" Then he
turned to his father. "Have you not reserved a blessing for
me?" he asked.

Isaac answered, "I have made [Jacob] your master, and
all his brethren I have given to him as servants; with grain
and wine I have sustained him. What shall I do now for
you, my son?"

For the first time in his life, the carefree Esau realized
that the blessing and birthright he thought had little value
were really very important. "Have you only one blessing,
my father? Bless me, even me also, O my father!" he said,
and he cried louder.

Then Isaac gave him this blessing:

> "Behold, your dwelling shall be of the fatness of
> the earth,
> And of the dew of heaven from above.
> By your sword you shall live,
> And you shall serve your brother;
> And it shall come to pass, when you become
> restless,
> That you shall break his yoke from your neck"
> (Genesis 27:39, 40).

Because Jacob had cheated him, Esau hated his younger
brother and said, "The days of mourning for my father are
at hand; then I will kill my brother Jacob."

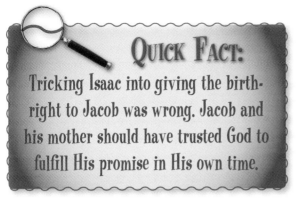

QUICK FACT:

Tricking Isaac into giving the birthright to Jacob was wrong. Jacob and his mother should have trusted God to fulfill His promise in His own time.

Rebekah heard this threat, and she began to plan for Jacob's escape. She remembered her home in Haran where her brother Laban lived. She told her son that he must leave his father's tents and make the long journey to Haran. After a while, Esau would forget the birthright and not be angry anymore. Then Jacob could come back home.

Father Isaac did not know of Esau's threat to kill Jacob, but he was anxious that Jacob should not marry a daughter of the people who worshiped idols. Esau had married daughters of the people of Canaan, and it had brought great sadness to his father and mother.

Isaac remembered the instruction of his father Abraham, and he was determined that Jacob should marry a daughter of his own people. He instructed Jacob to go to Haran and find a wife.

Jacob loved his home, and it was a sad day for him when he started out alone on his trip. He was worried, too, because he knew he had cheated his brother and stolen his blessing. He could not even guess how he would suffer for all the wrongs he had done to Esau.

JACOB FLEES FOR HIS LIFE

Genesis 28:10–31:23

J acob was a frightened man when he left his father's tents in Beersheba. He had never been far from home, and now he must travel more than four hundred miles on foot. On the first day, he walked quickly for several hours along the road that led away from everything familiar to him. He had good reason to hurry, since his brother, Esau, might follow and take revenge on him. Jacob knew that Esau traveled over this country on some of his hunting trips. He might have imagined that the hunter was hiding behind a tree or a rock along the trail, ready to shoot an arrow at him.

As the lonely man hurried along the road in a country that was new and strange to him, he thought of the roving tribes of fighting men living in the hills, who might attack him.

One evening, as the sun was setting, he came to a place where other travelers had stopped. Jacob did not know it, but Abraham had stopped there many years before, when he first entered the land of Canaan.

Weary from his travel, Jacob lay down on the ground with only a round stone for a pillow. Many times during the days since he had said Goodbye to his father and mother, he must have thought about the wrong he had done and the trouble it caused.

He felt fear as he went to sleep, but as he slept, Jacob had a wonderful dream. He saw a ladder, or a flight of steps, bright and shining, reaching from earth all the way to heaven. On the steps, angels were walking up and down. Standing over Jacob was the Lord, who said, "I am the Lord God of Abraham your father and the God of Isaac; the land on which you lie I will give to you and your descendants. Also your descendants shall be as the dust of the earth; you shall spread abroad to the west and the east, to the north and the south; and in you and in your seed all the families of the earth shall be blessed. Behold, I am with you and will keep you wherever you go, and will bring you back to this land; for I will not leave you until I have done what I have spoken to you."

Jacob woke up. The darkness seemed very close around him, because the bright angels of his dream had disappeared and only the dim outline of the hills could be seen. He looked up at the stars shining in all their beauty, and he said, "Surely the Lord is in this place, and I did not know it!"

As he thought of the glory of his dream, Jacob was afraid. He said: "How awesome is this place! This is none other than the house of God, and this is the gate of heaven!"

Early in the morning Jacob got up. He took the stone he had used as his pillow and set it up as a monument. He poured some oil on it, which was the custom in making a holy place of worship. Until then, that place had been called Luz, but Jacob named it Bethel, which means "the house of God."

As he stood there in the cool morning air, he made a promise to the Lord: "If God will be with me, and keep me in this way that I am going, and give me bread to eat and clothing to put on, so that I come back to my father's house in peace, then the Lord shall be my God. And this stone which I have set as a pillar shall be God's house, and of all that You give me I will surely give a tenth to You."

By this promise, Jacob said that he would be faithful to God. He would give God a tenth, or tithe, of all the wealth

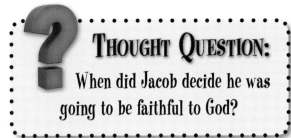

he gained. His grandfather Abraham had given tithe to the priest of Salem after he had rescued Lot and his family, and Isaac had told his son that it was a sacred duty to give a tenth to God.

No doubt much of the fear and loneliness Jacob had felt left him as he went on his journey from Bethel. Days passed into weeks before he arrived at Haran. As he came near the town, he saw a well by the side of the road, and near the well were three flocks of sheep. Jacob stopped and asked the men where they lived. The men said they were from Haran.

"Do you know Laban the son of Nahor?" asked Jacob.

The men replied, "We know him."

"Is he well?" he asked them.

"He is well," they said. "And look, his daughter Rachel is coming with the sheep."

Jacob turned and saw a beautiful young woman walking toward him. It was his cousin Rachel. He saw that her herd of sheep was thirsty, so he rolled the stone from the top of the well and watered the sheep. Then he went to Rachel and told her that he was Jacob, her cousin, the son of her father's sister, Rebekah. Jacob kissed Rachel, and tears came to his eyes because he was so happy to see a relative after his long, tiring journey.

Rachel ran home and told her father. Laban came out to meet Jacob, put his arms around him, and welcomed him into his house. Jacob stayed with Laban and began getting to know his sons and his two daughters, Rachel and Leah. When Jacob started to help his uncle take care of the flocks and herds, Laban noticed that his nephew knew how to care for the sheep and that he did his work faithfully.

After the son of Isaac and Rebekah had stayed in Haran for a month, Laban said, "Because you are my relative, should you therefore serve me for nothing? Tell me, what should your wages be?"

Jacob had fallen in love with Rachel, and he hoped that someday he might marry her. In reply to Laban's question, he said, "I will serve you seven years for Rachel your younger daughter."

It was the custom in those days for a man to pay a sum of money or to give cattle or a piece of land to the father of his bride as a dowry. Jacob did not have rich presents to give Laban, like the ones Abraham's servant, Eliezer, gave when he took Rebekah from the family years before. Therefore, he offered to work for seven years for his bride.

Laban thought this was a good bargain, so he said, "It is better that I give her to you than that I should give her to another man. Stay with me."

Seven years Jacob worked for his uncle, and the time passed

QUICK FACT:
Laban tricked Jacob into marrying Leah. Now Jacob knew what it felt like to be lied to and have something stolen from him.

quickly, because he was deeply in love with Rachel. At last the day came for the wedding. Laban's servants prepared a feast for the friends of the family, and everyone was merry. Jacob was a happy bridegroom.

During the evening, as was the custom of the country, Laban brought the bride to Jacob. The girl had a heavy veil over her face, and no one could see her, not even her husband, until the ceremony was over.

When the time came that Jacob could see his wife, he had a terrible surprise. It was not the beautiful Rachel who was his bride but her elder sister, Leah. Laban had deceived Jacob! Seven years he had worked, and he did not have the girl he loved to be his wife.

Jacob went to Laban and said, "What is this you have done to me? Was it not for Rachel that I served you? Why then have you deceived me?" In his heart Jacob must have remembered how he had cheated his own brother years before. He was beginning to reap what he had sown.

Laban told Jacob it was not proper for the younger daughter to marry before the older one. But he agreed that if Jacob would work another seven years, he could also have Rachel for his wife. It was often the custom of those times for men to have more than one wife. So, Rachel became his second wife, and Jacob stayed and worked for Laban another seven years.

After fourteen years away from Beersheba, Jacob was anxious to return to the home of his father and mother in the land of Canaan. By now, Jacob had eleven sons and a daughter along with his two wives, and he wished to take his family home. He said to Laban, "Send me away, that I may go to my own place and to my country."

Laban had been blessed with success while Jacob was with him, and he did not want his son-in-law to leave. So, Jacob worked six more years, and Laban paid him with flocks of sheep and herds of cattle.

Now Jacob's sheep and cattle increased rapidly, and he became wealthy. The sons of Laban became jealous, and they complained, saying, "Jacob has taken away all that was our father's, and from what was our father's he has acquired all this wealth." This was not true, because the Lord had been good to Jacob and had given him riches. But when Jacob saw that Laban's sons were jealous, he knew he should leave.

While Laban was away from home shearing his sheep, Jacob decided it was a good time to start on the journey. If he waited to tell his father-in-law goodbye, Laban would do everything he could to make him stay. Quickly Jacob put his two wives, his eleven sons, and his daughter on camels. With his flocks and herds driven by servants, the caravan started south toward Canaan, the land of his birth.

GOD SAYS:

"Then the Lord said to Jacob, 'Return to the land of your fathers and to your family, and I will be with you.' " —Genesis 31:3

Jacob was another pioneer. Like Abraham, his grandfather, he was willing to face danger to make his home in the land the Lord had promised to him. But there were some dangers ahead that even Abraham did not have to face. Jacob remembered how he had cheated his brother, Esau, by stealing his birthright. Would the hunter forget the old wrong, or would he be waiting to kill Jacob?

The pioneer had something else to worry him. He was leaving Laban's home without saying goodbye. His father-in-law would certainly be angry. Would he come after him? Jacob thought about these things as the caravan moved slowly along the mountain roads and into the desert country. Sometimes he wished he could hurry so Laban would not follow him. Then again, he wished he might go more slowly in order not to face Esau so soon.

The day came when the camels and the sheep and cattle were safely across the Euphrates River. The caravan was making good progress toward the land of Canaan. But soon Jacob heard news that troubled him. Laban was coming after him and would soon overtake his family.

A Fight in the Dark

Genesis 31:22–33:16

Not until three days after Jacob left Haran with all his family and possessions did Laban hear the news that his son-in-law had gone away. He was angry and started out immediately in pursuit of Jacob's caravan. Over the mountain roads and across the desert, Laban and his men hurried. They traveled for seven days before they saw the tents of Jacob pitched near Mount Gilead.

The night before Laban reached Jacob's camp, he was warned in a dream not to force Jacob to return to Haran. God said, "Be careful that you speak to Jacob neither good nor bad."

Laban's anger was cooled by these words. When he met Jacob the next morning, he said, "What have you done, that you have stolen away unknown to me, and carried away my daughters like captives taken with the sword? Why did you flee away secretly, and steal away from me, and not tell me; for I might have sent you away with joy and songs, with timbrel and harp? And you did not allow me to kiss my sons and my daughters. Now you have done foolishly in so doing. It is in my power to do you harm, but the God of your father spoke to me last night, saying, 'Be careful that you speak to Jacob neither good nor bad.' And now you have surely gone because you greatly long for your father's house."

Jacob knew that his father-in-law would not have allowed him to leave so easily if he had told him goodbye at Haran. So he answered Laban, "I was afraid, for I said, 'Perhaps you would take your daughters from me by force.' "

Then Laban complained to Jacob that his family idols had been stolen. Laban lived in a place where the people worshiped many gods, and he had heathen images in his home. Jacob told Laban that he had not taken them. He did not know that his wife Rachel had stolen the images and hidden them in the saddlebags of her camel.

"What is my trespass? What is my sin, that you have so hotly pursued me?" asked Jacob angrily. He reminded his father-in-law of the days and nights he had worked in winter and summer to care for Laban's sheep. Jacob had done this work faithfully and never taken anything that did not belong to him, yet Laban had not always paid him an honest wage. Jacob reminded him also that God had blessed Laban. He said, "Unless the God of my father, the God of Abraham and the Fear of Isaac, had been with me, surely now you would have sent me away empty-handed. God has seen my affliction and the labor of my hands, and rebuked you last night."

> **GOD SAYS:**
> "May the Lord watch between you and me when we are absent one from another." –Genesis 31:49

Then Laban and Jacob made peace, and they set up a stone as a monument in that place. The other men gathered stones to make a pile of rocks around the monument. Jacob called the place Mizpah, which means "watchtower." Laban said, "May the Lord watch between you and me when we are absent one from another." Jacob was grateful to God for saving him from serious trouble, and he offered a sacrifice and gave thanks to the Lord.

THOUGHT QUESTION:
How did Jacob know he was wrestling with an angel and not a man?

Laban and his men ate dinner with Jacob and camped nearby for the night. The next morning Laban told his daughters and his grandchildren goodbye and started on his journey back to Haran.

Jacob and his family traveled on through the desert country. They were nearing Canaan, and not far to the south was Edom, the land where Esau lived. Jacob well remembered the day more than twenty years before when he had cheated his brother out of the birthright. What could he do to show Esau he was sorry for his wrong act?

Jacob decided to send his servants to Esau to tell him that he was coming home with cattle and riches. The servants were told to beg for favor and kindness from Esau.

Soon the servants returned to Jacob with bad news. They told their master that Esau was coming to meet him with four hundred men. This seemed like a mighty army to helpless Jacob, and he was afraid for his family and for himself. What should he do? How could he save his wives and his children? With danger approaching, he turned to God and prayed.

"O God of my father Abraham and God of my father Isaac, the Lord who said to me, 'Return to your country and to your [family], and I will deal well with you': I am not worthy of the least of all the mercies and of all the truth which You have shown Your servant. . . . Deliver me, I pray, from the hand of my brother, from the hand of Esau; for I fear him. . . . For You said, 'I will surely treat you well, and make your descendants as the sand of the sea, which cannot be numbered for multitude.' "

From his flocks and herds Jacob took 220 goats, 220 sheep, 30 camels, 40 cows, and 10 bulls and sent them ahead to Esau as a present. When night came, Jacob moved his family across the river Jabbok, but he stayed behind alone to pray. He stood in a lonely spot in the mountains, and wild animals were near.

Suddenly a man came up to Jacob in the darkness. He felt a strong arm laid on him, and fear came over him. He was sure an enemy was trying to kill him. Jacob fought for his life with all his strength. For hours the struggle continued.

As the sky began to get light, the Stranger touched Jacob's hip and crippled him. Although he was suffering severe pain, the pioneer held on while the Stranger said, "Let Me go, for the day breaks."

But Jacob, who now realized he was wrestling with a heavenly Being, said, "I will not let You go unless You bless me!"

"What is your name?" asked the Stranger.

"Jacob," he replied.

"Your name shall no longer be called Jacob, but Israel; for you have struggled with God and with men, and have prevailed." The name *Israel* means "struggle with God."

The Stranger from heaven blessed Jacob, and Jacob called the place Peniel, which means "face of God." He

said, "I have seen God face to face, and my life is preserved."
Now there was courage in Jacob's heart, because he knew
that the Lord was with him in his time of trouble and had
given him a special blessing.

When the sun rose in the sky, Jacob made his way across the river to the camp, where his wives and children were waiting for him. He limped as he walked, for he had been injured while wrestling with the heavenly One.

Soon Jacob saw his brother marching toward him with his army of four hundred men. The pioneer arranged his family in separate groups to protect them, and then he went to meet Esau, limping in pain as he walked. The women and children stood watching. Would the brothers fight? Would Esau try to kill his twin?

Jacob stopped in the road and bowed before his brother seven times, an honor due to a chief in the country. Esau ran to meet Jacob and threw his arms around him. The old hatred was forgotten, and the brothers loved each other.

Then Esau looked around. "Who are these with you?" he asked, pointing to the women and children.

They are "the children whom God has graciously given your servant," Jacob replied as he introduced Esau to his family. Esau asked why the cattle, sheep, and other animals had been sent to him, and Jacob explained that they were a present.

At first the man from Edom refused to accept them. "I have enough, my brother," Esau said. "Keep what you have for yourself." With much urging, Esau finally agreed to keep the animals his brother had given him.

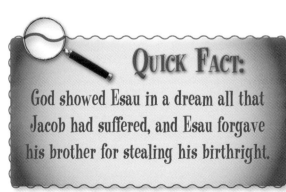

QUICK FACT:
God showed Esau in a dream all that Jacob had suffered, and Esau forgave his brother for stealing his birthright.

JOSEPH THE DREAMER

Genesis 37

Jacob made his home at Hebron, pitching his tents in the shade of the oak trees. Since he was growing old, he spent much of his time during the day at the door of his tent, resting on rugs and cushions. He was the chief of his people, and his twelve sons were in charge of the sheep and cattle and goats that grazed in the meadows and on the hillsides. Jacob's sons were named Reuben, Simeon, Levi, Judah, Dan, Naphtali, Gad, Asher, Issachar, Zebulun, Joseph, and Benjamin. Joseph and Benjamin were the sons of Rachel and the youngest boys in the family. They were Jacob's favorites.

Joseph was honest and stronghearted, a young man who could be depended on. His father loved to walk with him through the fields, telling him about God and how the world was created.

Joseph liked to play with his younger brother, Benjamin. The boys helped, as shepherds' sons often did, by filling snake holes so the sheep would not step in them and break a leg. Sometimes they might draw water from the well for the cattle.

Jacob's ten older sons were not good men. They were selfish and quarrelsome, and often they told lies and deceived their father. When Joseph saw his brothers doing wrong, it troubled him, and he tried to get them to do right; but they only hated him for his words of reproof.

To show Joseph how much he loved him, Jacob gave him a beautiful robe of fine cloth. The coat had many bright colors woven into it, and any boy in those days would have been proud to own it. Most of the shepherd boys wore only a plain shirt and a leather girdle. It was a special honor for Joseph to wear this bright coat and parade it before his brothers. But his father Jacob was not wise to show more love for one son than the others; and Joseph did wrong to show off in front of his brothers. When the ten brothers saw him in the beautiful coat, they scowled and hated him in their hearts in the same way Cain once hated Abel.

At the time of harvest Joseph helped cut the grain and bind it in sheaves. One night when he was seventeen years old, he had a dream. The next morning he told it to his brothers. He said, "Please hear this dream which I have dreamed: There we were, binding sheaves in the field. Then behold, my sheaf arose and also stood upright; and indeed your sheaves stood all around and bowed down to my sheaf."

This dream made his brothers angry, and they said scornfully, "Shall you indeed reign over us? Or shall you indeed have dominion over us?"

A few nights later, Joseph had a second dream, and again he told it to his brothers. He told them that in his dream he saw the bright sun, the silver moon, and eleven stars, shining in the heavens. As he watched, he said, he saw in his dream the sun, moon, and stars bow before him.

JOE MANISCALCO

Joseph's older brothers felt jealous of him. They hated him more and more because of his dreams and because he was proud of his beautiful coat that he wore so they had to look at it. When Jacob heard of his son's dreams, he wondered if God was telling the family that Joseph would someday become someone great.

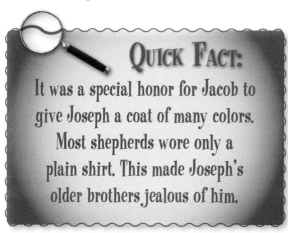

QUICK FACT:

It was a special honor for Jacob to give Joseph a coat of many colors. Most shepherds wore only a plain shirt. This made Joseph's older brothers jealous of him.

During the hot summer days the grass dried up in the meadows, and the ten older brothers drove the flocks of sheep to the north, where there was better pasture. After they had been gone for some time, Jacob was anxious to know how they were getting along. He called Joseph to his tent and told him he wanted to hear from his ten sons.

"Are not your brothers feeding the flock in Shechem? Come, I will send you to them," the father said to Joseph.

"Here I am," he replied.

Jacob commanded his son, "Please go and see if it is well with your brothers and well with the flocks, and bring back word to me."

The teenager was excited about going on an adventure. He had never been far from home, and now he was going on a journey of about fifty miles. It was a long distance in those days, because you either walked or rode on a slow-moving donkey.

Thinking he would have fun, Joseph left his father's tents and made his way over the hills and through the valleys until he came to Shechem. When he arrived at the town, he could not find his brothers. A man found Joseph searching in the fields and asked him, "What are you seeking?"

"I am seeking my brothers," Joseph replied. "Please tell me where they are feeding their flocks."

The man said, "They have departed from here, for I heard them say, 'Let us go to Dothan.' "

Joseph found the road to Dothan and walked the fifteen miles farther. From a hilltop he saw his brothers with their flocks of sheep. Although he had already trudged many miles, he ran down the slope, waving and shouting to them.

When the brothers saw Joseph coming across the fields, they began to talk about him. They made fun of his dreams and sneered at his beautiful coat. Some of the brothers who hated Joseph the most suggested they should kill him.

"Look, this dreamer is coming!" they said to one another. "Come therefore, let us now kill him and cast him into some pit; and we shall say, 'Some wild beast has devoured him.' We shall see what will become of his dreams!"

Reuben, the oldest, was more kindhearted than the other brothers. He said, "Shed no

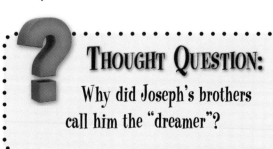

THOUGHT QUESTION:
Why did Joseph's brothers call him the "dreamer"?

blood, but cast him into this pit which is in the wilderness, and do not lay a hand on him."

While the brothers were arguing, Joseph came running up. The men did not greet him with words of welcome. Instead, they grabbed him roughly, threw him on the ground, and tore his colorful coat. The boy cried and begged for mercy, but his cruel brothers would not listen. They picked him up and threw him into a deep cistern, which, fortunately, did not have water in it.

Then the hardhearted men sat down to eat lunch. Reuben did not want to hear Joseph's cries for help, so he left

his brothers for a while. He intended to come back later and rescue his young brother. But while he was gone, a caravan of Ishmaelite traders came along the road, and the other brothers plotted a terrible crime.

When the brother named Judah saw the camels loaded with precious goods, he said, "What profit is there if we kill our brother and conceal his blood? Come and let us sell him to the Ishmaelites, and let not our hand be upon him."

The caravan came near, and the brothers hailed the leader. They offered to sell Joseph to him as a slave. The crafty merchant looked at the strong teen and offered to buy him for twenty pieces of silver. The brothers agreed, and Joseph was bound with ropes and carried away by the traders.

As the caravan of camels disappeared over the hills, there may have been some guilty looks on the faces of the brothers. They had sold their younger brother to be a slave, a fate often worse than death.

Later, Reuben returned to help Joseph out of the deep pit. But when he called out, there was no answer. *Where was Joseph?*

Worried at the disappearance of the boy, Reuben ran to his brothers, saying, "The lad is no more; and I, where shall I go?"

The brothers explained what they had done, and they became afraid. How could they go home and face their father? What would they say had happened to Joseph? In an attempt to deceive Jacob, they took the beautiful but ripped-up coat and dipped it in the blood of a goat. Then they started toward home, dreading the time when they would have to face their father.

As they came near their father's tents, he was waiting for them. He asked them if they had seen Joseph. Giving the bloodstained coat to Jacob, they said, "We have found this. Do you know whether it is your son's tunic or not?" They tried to cover up their crime with a lie.

The aged pioneer, who dearly loved Joseph, looked at the coat and touched it with trembling hands. Then he cried out, "It is my son's tunic. A wild beast has devoured him. Without doubt Joseph is torn to pieces."

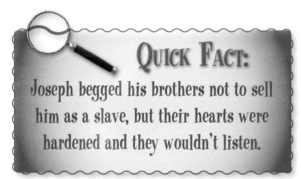

QUICK FACT:

Joseph begged his brothers not to sell him as a slave, but their hearts were hardened and they wouldn't listen.

As was the custom of the country when a person was in sorrow, Jacob tore his clothing and put on a rough cloth called sackcloth. For days he sat in his tent, mourning for his lost son.

Day after day the ten brothers heard the cries of their father, and they knew that their evil deed had broken his heart. They spoke to him, but Jacob refused to be comforted.

Away from their father, the brothers may have said to one another, "Well, we have gotten rid of Joseph. We can forget about him now! Nothing will come of his dreams, that's for sure."

But God was watching over Joseph, and, as the years went by, the brothers found out that they could never forget him!

A SLAVE IN PRISON

Genesis 39; 40

Joseph trudged along the dusty road with the camel caravan of the Ishmaelites. Tears filled his eyes as he thought of his home at Hebron. He looked at the hills to the east and knew that his father's tents were nearby, because the caravan was following a road that was only a few miles from his home. He had been loved and honored all his life, but now he was a slave. He had learned to have faith in God, and in this hour of trouble he prayed for help. He determined to be strong and do what was right, because his father had always trusted him.

The caravan took the road along the seashore, and after a while Joseph found out that the traders were heading for Egypt. This news made him heartsick, because Egypt was a strange, foreign land, and he knew his chances of ever returning home were growing less with every mile he traveled.

The day came when the camel train arrived at the frontier wall, where there was a strong fort. The Egyptian guards opened and inspected all the bundles the camels carried. When everything had been checked, the caravan moved on into the land of the Nile River.

Egypt presented many strange sights to Joseph. He saw temples, great pyramids, horses and chariots, and swift sail boats on the broad river. When the caravan reached the capital city, the traders sold Joseph to Potiphar, the captain of the king's guard. Even as a slave, Joseph decided that he would work faithfully and do his best to please his master.

The young man learned to speak the language of Egypt, and he did his work so well that Potiphar put him in charge of his house and all his property. God was with Joseph, and the king's officer was pleased to find a slave who could be trusted.

Joseph held his position in Potiphar's house for ten years, and then a severe test came to him. Potiphar's wife, an immoral woman, tried to get Joseph to do wrong. But the young man loved God and remained faithful to Him.

When he refused her suggestions, the woman turned against him, and she told lies and made false accusations about Joseph to her husband. Potiphar believed his wife and became angry. He had Joseph sent to prison.

Days and weeks passed, and no one came to help the young man who sat chained in a dark prison. He had no friends or relatives in the country to help him. But in spite of this unfair punishment, Joseph determined to obey God and do right.

After a while the jailer noticed Joseph and gave him work to do. He proved honest and dependable in all that he did, and the jailer found that he could trust him with many prison duties.

One day great excitement arose at the prison. Two important officials of the palace were imprisoned by order of Pharaoh, the Egyptian king. The two officers were Pharaoh's butler and baker. The butler prepared all the wine for Pharaoh, and the baker made all his bread and cakes. Pharaoh had somehow become angry with these men and had banished them to prison.

Joseph was given the task of caring for the new prisoners. One morning when he came to visit the butler and the baker in the cell they shared, he saw that they were unhappy. "Why do you look so sad today?" he asked.

THOUGHT QUESTION:

The Bible says that the Lord was with Joseph and made him successful. Why did the Lord help Joseph so much?

"We each have dreamed a dream," they replied, "and there is no interpreter of it."

Joseph said to them, "Do not interpretations belong to God? Tell them to me, please."

So the butler of Pharaoh told Joseph his dream. "Behold, in my dream," he said, "a vine was before me, and in the vine were three branches; it was as though it budded, its blossoms shot forth, and its clusters brought forth ripe grapes. Then Pharaoh's cup was in my hand; and I took the grapes and pressed them into Pharaoh's cup, and placed the cup in Pharaoh's hand."

Joseph listened closely to the butler's words. He remembered the dreams he had had as a teenager at home. God was with Joseph and immediately made the meaning of this dream clear to him. He said to the butler, "This is the interpretation of it: The three branches are three days. Now within three days Pharaoh will lift up your head and restore you to your place, and you will put Pharaoh's cup in his hand according to the former manner, when you were his butler."

Then the baker was anxious to tell his dream to Joseph, because he had heard the good words spoken to the butler. He said to Joseph, "I also was in my dream, and there I had three white baskets on my head. In the uppermost basket there were all kinds of baked goods for Pharaoh, and the birds ate them out of the basket on my head."

When Joseph heard the dream, he was sad. But he courageously told the baker the truth, although he knew it would bring him great sorrow. Joseph said, "This is the interpretation of it: The three baskets are three days. Within three days Pharaoh will lift off your head from you and hang you on a tree; and the birds will eat your flesh from you."

Three days later, Pharaoh was celebrating his birthday with a great feast. He sent for the butler and the baker and considered their cases. He restored the butler to his royal position, but the baker was hanged. Thus Joseph's words proved true, because God was with him.

Before the butler left the prison, Joseph asked a favor of him. The man would be working in the palace again, and he might be able to tell Pharaoh about any prisoner

> ## QUICK FACT:
> If Potiphar had truly believed his wife's story, Joseph would have been killed immediately. It was to protect Potiphar's reputation that Joseph was sent to prison.

who should be set free. "Remember me when it is well with you," Joseph said, "and please show kindness to me; make mention of me to Pharaoh, and get me out of this [prison]. For indeed I was stolen away from the land of the Hebrews; and also I have done nothing here that they should put me into the dungeon."

As Joseph watched the butler go back to the palace, he hoped that the man would remember him. But days, weeks, and months dragged by, and nothing happened. The butler had forgotten his promise made after Joseph's kindness. Behind the prison bars an innocent man still wondered when his prayers would be answered. Would he ever be set free from this Egyptian prison? A servant of the king of Egypt was in a position to speak a good word in his behalf, but he had not.

THOUGHT QUESTION:

How did Joseph know what the dreams of the baker and butler meant?

Joseph was homesick for his father's house. He longed to be free to return to the land of Canaan. As Joseph thought of his home, he prayed that God might use the butler to help him.

This is a good lesson in remembering a kind deed that a friend does for us. Too often we take favors for granted, and we forget to help others in their hour of need. The butler forgot his promise, and because of his neglect Joseph stayed many more months in prison.

FROM PRISON TO PALACE

Genesis 41

One morning, excitement and confusion spread through the palace of Pharaoh. The courtiers were alarmed, and the servants talked in whispers behind closed doors. Pharaoh was angry; he was shouting commands and making dreadful threats.

Now the butler heard what had happened. One of the servants told him that Pharaoh was troubled because of two strange dreams he'd had the night before. The dreams seemed to contain a special message for him and his country. Pharaoh was upset because he could not understand the meaning of the dreams.

While the butler did his work in the royal palace, he saw the wise men of the nation hurrying back and forth. Pharaoh had called them in to explain his dreams. He had told them the dreams, and they had searched diligently in books of magic for an answer; but they could find nothing to help the king.

Then the butler heard an angry shout, and the guards

led all of the wise men out of the court. The king had commanded the men to leave because they had failed to help him.

Again the servants talked together, and the courtiers met in the hallways of the palace. What could be done for their noble ruler? Suddenly the butler remembered his dream in prison and how Joseph had given him its true meaning. Yes, what Joseph had told the butler had actually happened; but the butler had forgotten his friend for two years! Quickly the butler walked to Pharaoh with a cup of wine. He told the king about Joseph and begged him to send for the prisoner.

GOD SAYS:

"So Joseph answered Pharaoh, saying, 'It is not in me; God will give Pharaoh an answer of peace.'" -Genesis 41:16

Now to call on a young foreigner in prison to tell Pharaoh the meaning of a dream was unheard of. But the king was desperate to find anyone who could tell him the truth. So he acted at once. Royal messengers ran to the prison and ordered the jailer to release Joseph so that he could go to the king's palace.

The son of Jacob was thrilled by the news. Perhaps he had hope of being freed. Joseph quickly prepared for this strange meeting. He shaved his face and head and dressed in spotless linen garments, as was the custom of the Egyptians.

Then the king's guards placed Joseph in a chariot, and the horses set off at a gallop. Upon arriving at the palace, he was led into the court, where Pharaoh sat upon a golden throne.

Joseph, who was now thirty years old, looked at the ruler with wonder. The king of Egypt wore a high crown on which was fastened a gold snake. On his hand was a ring, a sign of royal power. At the sides of the magnificent throne stood courtiers, officers, and a guard of soldiers. It was a breathtaking moment for Joseph, but he stood fearlessly awaiting the king's words.

"I have dreamed a dream," Pharaoh said to Joseph, "and there is no one who can interpret it. But I have heard it said of you that you can understand a dream, to interpret it."

"God will give Pharaoh an answer of peace," Joseph answered, making sure that the king understood he did not have wisdom in himself to interpret the dreams.

Then the ruler told Joseph what he had dreamed. He said, "In my dream, I stood on the bank of the river. Suddenly seven cows came up out of the river, fine looking and fat; and they fed in the meadow. Then behold, seven other cows came up after them, poor

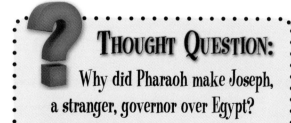

THOUGHT QUESTION: Why did Pharaoh make Joseph, a stranger, governor over Egypt?

and very ugly and gaunt, such ugliness as I have never seen in all the land of Egypt. And the gaunt and ugly cows ate up the first seven, the fat cows. When they had eaten them up, no one would have known that they had eaten them, for they were just as ugly as at the beginning. So I awoke.

"Also I saw in my dream, and suddenly seven heads [of grain] came up on one stalk, full and good. Then behold, seven heads [of grain], withered, thin, and blighted by the east wind, sprang up after them. And the thin heads devoured the seven good heads."

When he had spoken these words, Pharaoh waited for a reply.

Joseph, pale from his long imprisonment, looked at the monarch on his throne. He told Pharaoh that his two dreams had the same meaning. God was showing Pharaoh what was about to happen to his country. The seven fat cows and the seven plump ears of grain represented the next seven years, when Egypt would have good crops and rich harvests. But after that would come seven years of terrible famine, represented by the thin cows and the small ears of grain.

Pharaoh listened to every word Joseph spoke. He saw in this prisoner a man of strength and ability, a man who had faith in God.

After Joseph had revealed the meaning of the dreams, he continued speaking: "Now therefore, let Pharaoh select a discerning and wise man, and set him over the land of Egypt. Let Pharaoh do this, and let him appoint officers over the land, to collect one-fifth of the produce of the land of Egypt in the seven plentiful years. And let them gather all the food of those good years that are coming, and store up grain under the authority of Pharaoh, and let them keep food in the cities. Then that food shall be as a reserve for the land for the seven years of famine which shall be in the land of Egypt, that the land may not perish during the famine."

When he had said this he bowed and stood in his place. Pharaoh sat in thought for a moment and then said to his courtiers, "Can we find such a one as this, a man in whom is the Spirit of God?" Then, turning to Joseph, he said, "You shall be over my house, and all my people shall be ruled according to your word; only in regard to the throne will I be greater than you. . . . See, I have set you over all the land of Egypt."

Joseph must have felt as if he were in a dream. Only a few hours before, he had been sitting in the dark dungeon, and now he was a royal official next to Pharaoh himself! The king took the ring from his finger and put it on the hand of Joseph. He commanded that the newly appointed official be dressed in beautiful robes from the king's wardrobe and that a golden chain be put around his neck.

QUICK FACT:
God was able to use Joseph to not only save all Egypt from starvation, but his family back in Canaan too.

A royal chariot drawn by stately horses was presented to Joseph, and when he, as the new governor of the land, rode through the streets or along the country roads, servants ran before him shouting for the people to bow in homage to him.

Soon Joseph made a trip throughout the land of Egypt. He saw how the Nile River rose and flooded the fields. He watched the Egyptians plowing, planting the grain, and preparing for the harvest.

During the next seven years the land was filled with plenty. Joseph directed that large storehouses be built, and so much grain was stored away in them that Joseph could not keep a complete account of it.

Joseph married an Egyptian maiden named Asenath, and they had two sons. Their first boy was called Manasseh, meaning "forgetfulness," because Joseph said God had helped him forget his imprisonment and trouble. Their second son was named Ephraim, meaning "fruitfulness," because God had made Joseph to prosper in Egypt.

When the seven years of abundant crops had passed, Joseph awaited the eighth year. Would famine come as he had told Pharaoh? At the time of year when the Nile River usually flooded the country, the water grew shallow instead. The land was not watered, and the grain withered and died in the fields. The grass turned brown and dried up so that the cattle had nothing to eat. Then the people of Egypt cried to Pharaoh for food, and the ruler said, "Go to Joseph; whatever he says to you, do."

The hungry, worried Egyptians came to Governor Joseph, and he was prepared to meet all their needs. He opened the huge storehouses and sold grain to the people. Thus, Joseph's years of hard work and planning were rewarded, and he saved the nation from starvation.

In the land of Canaan where Jacob and his eleven sons lived, there was a great famine and nothing was stored away. Soon Jacob's family would starve if he did not find a way to get food.

FOOD FOR THE HUNGRY

Genesis 42

O ne hot day in Canaan, when no rain had fallen for many months, Jacob called his sons to his tent. The meadows were brown and dry, the stalks of grain had withered in the dust, and wide cracks had appeared in the soil that was baked by the hot winds. Jacob and his sons knew that if the dry weather continued, the family would soon face starvation. The men were tired and hot from their work, and the threat of hunger caused them to cast worried glances at one another. Where could they get food for their wives and their children?

Jacob spoke sharply to his sons. "Why do you look at one another?" he said. "Indeed I have heard that there is grain in Egypt; go down to that place and buy for us there, that we may live and not die."

At the word *Egypt,* the ten brothers dropped their heads. The fact that they had sold Joseph many years before to traders heading to Egypt was still on their minds. Since that day the men had not talked about that country. And now their father was commanding them to go there to buy grain. Benjamin, the youngest brother, would stay behind, because Jacob was determined to protect the one son of Rachel that he had left.

The ten brothers could do nothing but obey their father's command. They set out with their pack animals on the road that led over the hills and through the desert. After a journey of several days, they came to the great fortress at the entrance to the land of Egypt. After the guards had inspected the travelers, they were allowed to pass into the country. They made their way along the highway to the capital city, where crowds of people were going to buy grain from the governor.

At the storehouse, the brothers found a place in the milling multitude and awaited their turn. When they arrived at the front of the line, the men made their request for grain to the royal officer.

Joseph recognized his brothers at once, but they did not notice that he was Joseph. He did not reveal his secret, but treated his brothers as strangers. He spoke to them in the language of Egypt, and his words were translated to Hebrew so they could understand.

GOD SAYS:

"Your servants are twelve brothers, the sons of one man in the land of Canaan; and in fact, the youngest is with our father today, and one is no more." –Genesis 42:13

"Where do you come from?" he asked them.

"From the land of Canaan to buy food," they said.

Joseph remembered

how his brothers had dumped him in the pit and later sold him as a slave. He wondered if they were as cruel and wicked as they had been twenty years earlier. To test them, he

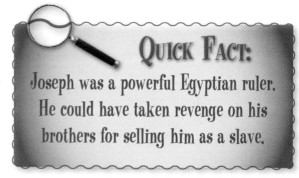

QUICK FACT:
Joseph was a powerful Egyptian ruler. He could have taken revenge on his brothers for selling him as a slave.

said roughly, "You are spies! You have come to see the nakedness of the land!"

But they denied this, saying, "Your servants are twelve brothers, the sons of one man in the land of Canaan; and in fact, the youngest is with our father today, and one is no more." By their words they revealed that they had never been able to forget about their missing brother, Joseph.

Acting like a stern governor, Joseph continued to accuse them of being spies. He said that the only way they could prove they were honest men was to send for their youngest brother. At a signal from Joseph, the Egyptian guard took the men to a dungeon, where they lay frightened and miserable.

After three days Joseph called his brothers before him again. He had a plan to test them to see if they were now true to their father. He said, "Do this and live, for I fear God: If you are honest men, let one of your brothers be confined to your prison house; but you, go and carry grain for the famine of your houses. And bring your youngest brother to me; so your words will be verified, and you shall not die."

The sons of Jacob talked among themselves in their own language after Joseph had spoken, and they did not know he could understand what they said. Reuben reminded them, "Did I not speak to you, saying, 'Do not sin against the boy'; and you would not listen? Therefore behold, his blood is now required of us."

When Joseph spoke to his brothers again, he commanded that Simeon be put in prison, and the other nine men were given bags of grain. But unknown to them, Joseph ordered that their money be placed in the top of their sacks.

THOUGHT QUESTION:

Why didn't Joseph tell his brothers who he was at first?

The sons of Jacob loaded their pack animals and started toward Canaan. They were silent and afraid because of what the governor had done, and they wondered how they would explain Simeon's imprisonment to their father.

At the end of the day they stopped at a camping place, and one of the brothers opened his sack to give his donkey some grain. When he looked in the bag, he gave a cry of surprise and distress. "My money has been restored, and there it is, in my sack!" he said to his brothers.

They were certain that this was a horrible mistake. They had been accused of being spies, and now here was proof that they were thieves. They hurried along on their homeward journey to tell their father what had happened.

In the door of Jacob's tent the nine sons gathered before the aged pioneer. They tried to tell him what had happened, but their father could not understand why Simeon had been left behind in prison. They told Jacob that they must take Benjamin with them on the next trip to Egypt, but he would not listen.

Then, to make matters worse, when the other men opened their bags, each one found his money in his sack. They had not paid for any of the grain that had been sold to them by the royal officer! Now they felt terrified. They never wanted to see Egypt again.

At the same time, Jacob was weeping for another lost son. He said, "You have bereaved me. . . . Joseph is no more, Simeon is no more, and you want to take Benjamin. . . . All these things are against me."

Reuben tried to reason with his father, saying that the governor would not see them if they did not bring Benjamin on the next trip. He promised that he would be responsible for the safety of the youngest son when they made the journey. But Jacob would not listen to his son's words. His words were firm: "My son shall not go down with you." And there the matter rested.

The nine sons left their father's tent and went to their wives and families. They were thankful to have food to eat, because the famine was severe. But as the brothers looked at the sacks of grain, they knew that soon it would be necessary for them to go to Egypt again. "Egypt!" They hated the word more than ever before!

JOSEPH FACES HIS BROTHERS

Genesis 43–45:24

N o rain fell in the land of Canaan, and the famine dragged on month after month. Jacob was thankful for the supply of food his sons had brought from Egypt. But every time the nine brothers went to get grain from the sacks, they thought of Simeon in prison in that far-away land.

The food supply was dwindling fast, and they knew they should soon start on another trip to Egypt. But they did not dare talk about it to their father. What would he say if they asked him to allow Benjamin to go with them?

The day came, however, when Jacob called his sons to his tent. "Go back, buy us a little food," he commanded.

Judah said to him, "The man solemnly warned us, say-ing, 'You shall not see my face unless your brother is with you.'"

The old man knew that Benjamin must go on the dan-gerous trip, but he bowed his head while Judah was speak-ing. "Send the lad with me," Judah said to his father Israel, "and we will arise and go, that we may live and not die, both we and you and also our little ones."

Jacob finally agreed, saying, "If it must be so." He instructed his sons to take presents to the governor in Egypt, some honey, nuts, spices, and myrrh. They were also to take the money to pay for the grain from the first trip along with money to buy more grain.

Then their aging father gave a final word of blessing, praying that God would take care of them on their perilous mission. He

THOUGHT QUESTION:

Why did Joseph keep putting the money back into his brothers' sacks?

said, "Take your brother also, and arise, go back to the man. And may God Almighty give you mercy before the man, that he may release your other brother and Benjamin."

The brothers made the journey to Egypt in good time, and again they were brought before Joseph, the royal officer in charge of selling grain. When he saw Benjamin with his brothers, Joseph commanded his servant to take the men to his home and prepare a meal for them. He would give them the best food he had.

Fear came into their hearts, however, when they saw that they were being taken to the royal officer's home. Would he punish them because of the money they had unknowingly taken in their sacks? When they arrived at the governor's house, the brothers spoke to the chief steward, who met them at the door.

"O sir," they said, "we indeed came down the first time

to buy food; but it happened, when we came to the encampment, that we opened our sacks, and there, each man's money was in the mouth of his sack, our money in full weight; so we have brought it back in our hand. And we have brought down other money in our hands to buy food. We do not know who put our money in our sacks."

The steward answered them kindly and told them not to be afraid. Soon their imprisoned brother Simeon was brought in, and they had a happy reunion. The brothers were amazed that they should be guests in the governor's home. They hurried to get their presents ready to give the governor at the noon meal.

When Joseph arrived, the men bowed low before him, and they gave him the gifts from their father Jacob. "Is your father well," he asked, "the old man of whom you spoke? Is he still alive?"

"Your servant our father is in good health; he is still alive," they said, bowing deeply to the governor again. Joseph must have been thinking about his boyhood dreams, when his brothers' sheaves and the sun, moon, and eleven stars bowed before him. But for now he would not tell them who he was, because he wanted to test them further to see if there was love in their hearts—the kind of love they did not have when they sold him as a slave. Looking at Benjamin, he asked, "Is this your younger brother of whom you spoke to me?" They assured him that he was.

The brothers were placed at one large table, and house servants brought in the food. Joseph ate at a table by himself, since it was not the custom of Egyptians to eat with foreigners. The eleven sons of Jacob were seated according to their age, from the oldest to the youngest. They were amazed that the governor should know the order of their birth. And the men had another surprise coming. While they ate, they noticed that Benjamin was given five times as much food and drink as they received.

Now Joseph had given a special command to his steward concerning the bags of grain. He told the steward to fill the sacks and put each man's money in the top of his sack, just as he had on the previous trip. In Benjamin's sack he was to put Joseph's silver cup.

Early the next morning the travelers set out on their journey toward home. They were happy because all eleven of them were returning to their father. But they had only gone a few miles from the city when Joseph's steward rode up and stopped them on the road. He accused Jacob's sons of stealing the governor's silver cup.

The brothers declared, "Why does my lord say these words? Far be it from us that your servants should do such a thing." They said that the one who had the cup in his possession should become a slave for life. To prove that they didn't have it, each one unloaded his sack and opened it for inspection.

The steward began his search with Reuben, the oldest son, and went on down the line, according to their ages. When the steward came to Benjamin's sack, he found the beautiful silver cup! The brothers were struck with grief and terror and tore their clothes. What could they do to save Benjamin? How would they answer to their father for another lost son?

Sick at heart, the men returned to the city and bowed low once more before the governor. "What deed is this you have done?" Joseph said to them.

A dreadful silence fell on the men for a moment, and then Judah stepped forward and said, "What shall we say to my lord? What shall we speak? Or how shall we clear ourselves? God has found out the iniquity of your servants; here we are, my lord's slaves, both we and he also with whom the cup was found."

Joseph exclaimed that it was only the man with the cup in his sack who would be his slave for life. "And as for you," he added, "go up in peace to your father."

Go to their father! Again the thought brought fear to the sons of Jacob. They knew how he had mourned years before

> **QUICK FACT:**
> During the years that Joseph had been separated from his brothers, they had become good, kind, honest men.

when he learned that Joseph was gone. Now he was advanced in years, and the news that Benjamin was a slave would surely cause the old man's death.

Judah then came near to the governor and told him of Jacob's love for his youngest son. He revealed his father's sorrow at having to say goodbye to Benjamin when they started on the trip to Egypt. As Judah spoke, Joseph saw that a wonderful change had taken place in the hearts of his brothers. They were not the same cruel, evil men who had sold him to the traveling merchants.

As a final plea, Judah said, "Now therefore, please let your servant remain instead of the lad as a slave to my lord, and let the lad go up with his brothers. For how shall I go up to my father if the lad is not with me, lest perhaps I see the evil that would come upon my father?"

When Joseph saw Judah's love for his father and for Benjamin, he could no longer hide himself from his brothers. He commanded all the Egyptian officials to leave the room, and then he began to cry. All the longing for home came back to the long-lost son in that moment. For twenty years he had been in a foreign country. Now the dream of seeing his father might come true! Stretching out his arms to his brothers, he said, "I am Joseph; does my father still live?"

The brothers could not say one word, their astonishment was so great. They stood in silent amazement. Joseph, their lost brother, was a ruler in Egypt! They began to feel afraid when they thought about their guilt and realized that Joseph could take revenge on them. Joseph suddenly realized how they felt, and he said, "Please come near to me."

When they were close to him, he said, "I am Joseph your brother, whom you sold into Egypt. But now, do not therefore be grieved or angry with yourselves because you sold me here; for God sent me before you to preserve life. For these two years the famine has been in the land, and there are still five years in which there will be neither plowing nor harvesting. And God sent me before you to preserve a posterity for you in the earth, and to save your lives by a great deliverance."

The brothers could hardly believe what they heard. Joseph was

God Says:

"Do not therefore be grieved or angry with yourselves because you sold me here; for God sent me before you to preserve life." –Genesis 45:5

forgiving them! He kissed them and spoke words of peace and comfort to them. Then they talked about all the things that had happened during the years Joseph had been absent from home.

The news that Joseph's brothers were in the city found its way to Pharaoh, and he was pleased about it. Joseph went and appeared before the king's throne, and Pharaoh said to him, "Say to your brothers, 'Do this: Load your [animals] and depart; go to the land of Canaan. Bring your father and your households and come to me; I will give you the best of the land of Egypt, and you will eat the fat of the land.' " He urged Joseph to give carts to his brothers, so they could move their families and their father to Egypt and enjoy its riches.

Soon the eleven brothers were on their way home once more. This time they had wagons to bring all their possessions back to Egypt. They carried back to Canaan many gifts Joseph had given them, and some for Jacob too. They remembered Joseph's message to his father, how he had told them to say, "God has made me lord of all Egypt; come down to me, do not tarry. You shall dwell in the land of Goshen, and you shall be near to me, you and your children, your children's children, your flocks and your herds, and all that you have."

As the eleven sons made their way across the desert, they wondered if Jacob would believe them when they told him Joseph was alive. Now they must tell their father how they had sold Joseph and lied and deceived him many years before. It would not be easy to reveal all of this to Jacob and ask him to forgive them.

FATHER AND SON MEET

Genesis 45:25–47:31

Jacob waited anxiously at Hebron for the return of his sons. For him the days passed slowly, and he sent his servants out many times to watch for the travelers. At last the day came when a servant ran to tell him that his sons were approaching. Jacob left his tent and stood watching as the caravan crossed the field. He counted the boys when they were near enough to be seen. There were ten, eleven— yes, eleven! He saw smiles on their faces too. *They must have been successful on their journey,* he thought.

The brothers came on ahead of the caravan, and Jacob saw that they were excited about something. They all began to speak at once. "Joseph is still alive, and he is governor over all the land of Egypt," they told him.

The words stunned the aging father, and he could not understand what his sons were talking about. They repeated the words over and over. They told him how they had sold Joseph years before, and they asked him to forgive them for their evil deed. Then they brought out the presents Joseph

154

had sent, and they showed him the wagons that were to take the father and all his possessions to their new home in the land of the Nile.

When Jacob realized that Joseph was alive, he was ready to move from his home. He said, "It is enough. Joseph my son is still alive. I will go and see him before I die."

God sent the faithful man a message of courage. In a dream the Lord told Jacob not to be afraid to go to the land of Egypt, because his children would prosper and become a great nation. And he received the promise again that they would come back to Canaan.

QUICK FACT:
Pharaoh invited Joseph's brothers, their families, and his father Jacob to come live in Egypt.

Soon the baggage was loaded, and the whole family set out on their journey. Jacob's family numbered sixty-six people in Canaan, including the sons' wives and children. With Joseph, his wife, and their two children, the total number in Jacob's family was seventy people.

When the caravan came to the fortress at Egypt's frontier, the guard allowed it to pass through immediately. The soldiers had been told that the governor's family was coming to live in Egypt.

The wagons rolled on until they reached the land of Goshen. Joseph's messengers told him when the caravan was arriving, and he rode in his chariot to meet his father. It was a happy reunion when the long-lost son threw his arms around his aged father and cried.

"Now let me die," Israel said to Joseph, "since I have seen your face, because you are still alive."

Jacob and his sons made their home in the area of Goshen, a rich and well-watered part of Egypt. When Pharaoh heard that Joseph's family had arrived, he was anxious to meet Ja-

cob. The momentous day came when the aging pioneer and five of his sons were brought to the king's palace. There Jacob saw the magnificent building, the gold throne, the soldiers, and courtiers. He realized the greatness of Egypt, and he was proud that his son was governor, next to Pharaoh himself.

"How old are you?" Pharaoh asked Jacob.

"The days of the years of my pilgrimage are one hundred and thirty years," Jacob replied. "Few and evil have been the days of the years of my life." No doubt the man of God remembered some of the hardships—the flight from his home after he had cheated Esau, his years of work in Haran, the death of his dearest wife, and the loss of Joseph. But in spite of all this, Jacob counted his blessings. God had promised to make his children a strong nation.

Joseph was a busy man while the famine continued year after year. But, first of all, he made sure that his family had plenty of food

GOD SAYS:

"I will go down with you to Egypt, and I will also surely bring you up again."
-Genesis 46:4

and supplies in their new home. After the years of famine were over, Joseph continued his duties as a royal officer.

The sons of Jacob prospered in Egypt, and the family grew. But as the years passed, Jacob grew feeble and was nearing the end of his life. He sent for Joseph to come to his bedside and asked his son to promise that he would bury his father in the Cave of Machpelah, where Abraham and the other members of the family had been buried. Joseph promised that he would fulfill his father's request.

UNDER A CRUEL KING

Genesis 48–50; Exodus 1

When Jacob knew he was about to die, he called all his sons and Joseph's two sons to him and gave them each a special blessing. He reminded them how the Lord had been with him in all the years of his life, and he repeated the promise that the family would become a great nation.

When Jacob died, the people of Egypt observed a period of mourning for seventy days. Joseph had the body embalmed according to the custom of the Egyptians. After the days of mourning, Joseph asked Pharaoh for permission to go to his old home and bury his father in the Cave of Machpelah. The king readily granted the request, and a large funeral procession made the journey to Canaan. In it were the family of Jacob, the king's courtiers, and companies of soldiers on horseback.

Returning to Egypt after the burial of their father, the sons were afraid that Joseph might seek revenge on them for the way they had treated him years before. They thought he might have been waiting until his father died before punishing them. So, they approached Joseph and again asked his forgiveness.

Joseph said to them, "Do not be afraid, for am I in the place of God? But as for you, you meant evil against me; but God meant it for good, in order to bring it about as it is this day, to save many people alive. Now therefore, do not be afraid; I will provide for you and your little ones."

Joseph did not hate his brothers or try to get even with them for the way they had treated him. He saw how God had guided his life and had been with them through the years.

The brothers were happy at this assurance from Joseph, and the family prospered as the years passed. As long as Joseph lived, his brothers were honored in Egypt.

When he was 110 years old, Joseph knew he was about to die, so he called his extended family together and said to them, "I am dying; but God will surely visit you, and bring you out of this land to the land of which He swore to Abraham, to Isaac, and to Jacob."

After Joseph's death, other pharaohs came to the throne of Egypt,

GOD SAYS:
"So Joseph died, being one hundred and ten years old; and they embalmed him, and he was put in a coffin in Egypt." -Genesis 50:26

but they did not know anything about his fame and what he had done in saving the nation from famine. One pharaoh who became the country's ruler saw that the family of Jacob had grown rich and comfortable in the land of Goshen. Because he was afraid they might become more powerful than the Egyptians, he made harsh laws against them. They were no longer free to live on their farms and raise cattle and sheep. Now they must work as slaves for the king.

The powerful pharaoh planned great new cities. He ordered thousands of laborers to work building these cities for him. Some of the workmen were the descendants of Jacob. In large groups they were driven to work making bricks and carrying them to the builders. They labored from sunrise until dark, and there

THOUGHT QUESTION:

Why was the new Pharaoh afraid of the Israelites?

seemed no end to the work. In this time of oppressive slavery they remembered the promise made to Abraham, to Isaac, and to Jacob. They longed for the freedom of the land of Canaan, where their forefathers had lived.

God had not forgotten His promise. A day would come when all the children of Israel would be free and would return to their home in Canaan. The deliverance of the people from Egypt would become one of the greatest stories of all time. The brave adventurers before them had blazed the trail to the land of Canaan, but someday faithful men, who would be the conquerors of the land, would lead the people to their promised home.